Winter Search Party

Other Books by Helen Ross Russell

CITY CRITTERS
CLARION THE KILDEER

Winter Search Party

A GUIDE TO INSECTS AND OTHER INVERTEBRATES

by
Helen Ross Russell

Illustrations by
Viola Kohl Mohn

THOMAS NELSON INC.
New York / Camden

First edition

Library of Congress Catalog Card Number: 79–145927
ISBN 0–8407–6130–9 (trade); ISBN 0–8407–6131–7 (library)
Manufactured in the United States of America

To Bob, who has shared the joys of discovery and observation of scores of small animals in the winter world of mountaintops, farmland, city streets, and apartment-house window boxes.

Contents

chapter   page

I. **Getting Ready**   *13*
    An introduction to hunting invertebrate animals
    in winter.

II. **What's Inside That Building?**   *17*
    An imaginary collecting trip to discover the
    kinds of invertebrate animals that overwinter
    in unheated buildings will introduce you to
    collecting techniques and to a variety
    of animals.

III. **Housing for Small Animals**   *25*
    If you want to learn how the animals behave
    when they aren't hibernating, this chapter
    will tell you how to care for them.

IV. **Wooden Dormitories**   *31*
    The kinds of invertebrates that are most
    commonly found in logs and in dead
    wood are described here.

V. **An Egg Hunt**   *41*
    Many invertebrates overwinter as eggs.
    This will help you find some of them.

VI. Chickadee Punching Bags and
Squirrel Desserts   *51*

    Squirrels and birds can give you clues
    if you are hunting for insect pupae.

VII. Witches'-Brooms and Gingerbread
Houses   *59*

    Winter is a splendid time to start a
    gall collection.

VIII. A Well-Stocked Pantry   *71*

    Even though you cannot open a honeybee
    hive in winter, bees and their
    very interesting activities can be
    observed around a hive entrance.

IX. Seasonal Travelers   *79*

    These are the animals that you cannot observe
    during the winter because they have gone to
    warmer places.

X. Around the House   *85*

    You can hunt these invertebrates without
    putting on warm clothing.

XI. Business As Usual   *93*

    In spite of the temperature, many invertebrate
    animals can be found in a
    rapidly flowing brook.

XII. Ice Fishing   *103*

    Animals in lakes and ponds have to adapt
    to hard times.

XIII. Micro-Worlds   *111*

    You can have an exciting time with a gallon
    jar of pond water and a microscope.

XIV.   Mini-Habitats   123
       Many pond animals can be reared in aquariums
       in winter.

XV.   Surprise Packages   131
       Parasitic insects will be found living in
       every habitat and animal group.

XVI.   Creatures of the Snow   139
       Five kinds of insects that are active in the
       middle of winter.

XVII. An End and a Beginning   147
       A winter search party can lead to
       many other activities.

       Appendix   151
       What Animal Is This?
       A key to invertebrate animals.

       Bibliography   161

       Index   165

Note:
   Definitions of unfamiliar words will be
   found on the page where the
   word first appears. Check Index for this
   page number.

Winter Search Party

CHAPTER 1

Getting Ready

Have you ever looked out the window on a bright winter day and wondered where all the small animals went? All through the autumn there were flies and bees and wasps feeding on the chrysanthemums, asters, and other flowers. Earthworms were still coming up to the surface of the soil at night. Spiders were spinning webs. Praying mantises were catching any insects that ventured too close. Dragonflies were catching mosquitoes over the pond.

Then the temperature dropped. Frost killed the flowers; the soil froze; ice covered the pond. The little animals disappeared.

Where did they go? Did they migrate like birds, or hibernate like woodchucks and turtles? Or were they able to store food like squirrels? Finding the answers to these questions can lead to many adventures. You will have to be as keenly observant as a detective. You will need the inquiring spirit and imagination of a scientist.

You will not need much equipment. You can keep a couple of plastic bags in your pocket ready to pop specimens into. Small bottles and vials in which medi-

Equipment.

cines are sold are also fine for this purpose. You may
find a small pocketknife useful for lifting a specimen
out of a crack or cutting off a twig. A straight pin
can also be used for lifting tiny specimens or opening
small cocoons. Tweezers can be helpful in picking up
some animals. A flashlight is useful for examining
dark corners and narrow cracks. You will want a hand
lens for examining small specimens.

Warm clothes are important for outdoor work.
Gloves or mittens and boots, along with a hat that covers
your ears, will let you forget about the weather so you
can concentrate on your search. A notebook or a card
file is a must if you are going to do any research.

You can start anywhere, anytime. The first step in
the search is thinking. If you play hide-and-seek, you
know that the person who's "it" is more successful
if he knows something about the habits of the players
and thinks about them. He'll remember that Johnny

loves to climb so he'll look in high places for Johnny, or that Mary can't run fast and usually hides close to home base. And he'll see Jimmy's dog sticking his nose in the door of the old shed and wagging his tail; it's easy to find Jimmy when his dog is around. Perhaps he'll listen to the bluejays scolding; they tell him someone must be near their nest.

The same kind of thinking helps in this search. If the small animals were busy one bright autumn day and gone the next, as soon as the temperature dropped, they couldn't have gone far. Where could they have gone where they will be protected from the weather and safe from their enemies?

What shelters are near your home? Are there garages, sheds, barns? Are you near a park or a vacant lot? Is your cellar unfinished? How about the outside of buildings? Is there space behind a rainspout? Under a windowsill? On a porch? Around the trim? Under shingles? Are there cracks around the windows? Little animals do not need big hiding places. Do you know where there are piles of leaves? Clumps of grass? Stones or boards lying on the ground? Rotting logs?

Many birds that stay with us all winter are insect eaters. You can find insect hiding places by watching

More equipment.

Spider web with three silken spheres.

later, after you have learned more about the animal that made them. If you do, you can come back. Your label tells you how many you left behind and where they are.

You use your flashlight to examine the side of the window. Something is glistening. A lovely pale-green insect with golden eyes is clinging to the wall. When you touch it, it moves its long, slender antennae. You'd better put this one into a vial. It would be too bad to damage it.

There are mosquitoes here, too: two of them. You know you don't want any of them around next spring, so you collect them both.

Two mosquitoes.

LENGTH

You rake out a pile of leaves from one corner and find a prize: a brown-and-black woolly bear caterpillar, all curled up and with his tender under-parts covered.

There's a piece of canvas on the floor, too. Lift it up. It's not frozen. Unfold it, and between the layers you find two brown house crickets. They aren't exactly alike. One is larger and has wings. The smaller one has short pads where his wings should be. You decide to bring them both indoors.

There's something else, too—in the crack where the beam supporting the wall joins the floor. You see familiar long legs. It's a centipede. In summer, centipedes are hard to catch as they dash over the wall, and if, by chance, you grab one by a leg, he sheds it and hurries away on his other twenty-nine legs. Now, however, he is cold and stiff; you can pick him up easily.

Take the collection indoors, and have a good look at it and at your notes. You found:

LENGTH

Brown-and-black woolly bear caterpillar, curled up.

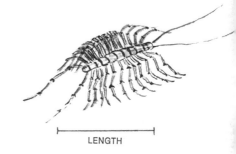

LENGTH

House centipede.

3 silken spheres
6 cocoons
2 house crickets
2 mosquitoes
1 pale-green creature with long slender antennae and beautiful golden eyes.
1 woolly bear caterpillar
1 centipede

You start by examining the silken sphere. Hold it with the tweezers and use a pin to separate the silk. Inside the outer cover is an even tighter, more closely woven sphere; and inside it are tiny spheres. Are they eggs? No, there are legs attached to each sphere and some of them are moving. Under the hand lens it is easy to see that they are baby spiders.

What about the cocoon? What's inside it? You open it and find two things: a brown cigar-shaped structure and a dried-up brown pellet about the size of a raisin. Look at the pellet with a hand lens. Can you see eye covers, mouthparts, six short legs, and a dried, wrinkled skin? Now look at the cigar-shaped object. It is covered with sculptured designs. Examine these designs carefully. Can you find places for eyes, wings, mouth, legs, antennae? Notice how different they are from the eye covers, legs, and mouthparts on the dried pellet. The pellet is the dried skin that was shed by a caterpillar after it had woven the cocoon. When it shed its skin, it lost its caterpillar form. It became a pupa. Inside the pupal skin it turns into a new form called a moth. The sculpturing on the outside of the pupal skin shows where the parts of the moth are developing.

We say insects that change in this way have complete metamorphosis. A metamorphosis is a change of form. Many young insects look entirely unlike their parents. A caterpillar does not look like the moth or butterfly it becomes. A maggot does not look like a fly. A young insect that looks different from its parents is called a larva (plural: larvae). To become an adult it goes into an inactive stage called a pupa (plural: pupae). Sometimes a pupa is in a silken or a papery cocoon. The body of the insect is entirely changed in the pupal stage. Wings usually develop. New mouthparts, antennae, and legs form, and reproductive organs develop. When an insect emerges from its pupal skin it is adult. It will never grow bigger, and it is ready to reproduce.

Crickets and some other insects, like grasshoppers, katydids, roaches, stink bugs, leafhoppers, and spittle bugs, have gradual metamorphosis. When they hatch they look like small copies of their parents, except that their heads are large for their bodies and they do not have wings. They are called nymphs.

As the nymphs feed, they shed their skins. This is called molting. The first time a nymph molts it develops little pads where its wings will be. Each time it molts the pads are larger. Finally, at the last molt, the insect has wings. It is no longer a nymph. It is an adult. It will not grow any larger or molt again. It is ready to reproduce.

An adult cricket and a cricket nymph were hiding in the canvas. If it had become very cold, the nymph would have died before spring came.

What about that pretty little green creature? By now it is quite warm. It is waving its long, slender antennae and moving its legs.

Like all the other creatures in this collection, it is

Two brown house crickets: (A) Adult; (B) Nymph.

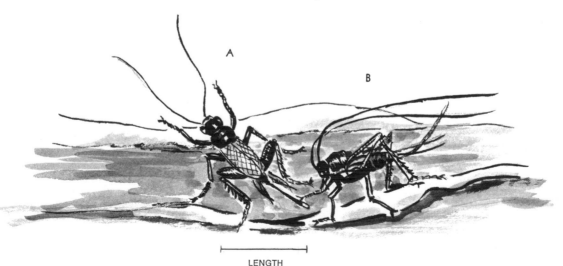

A

B

LENGTH

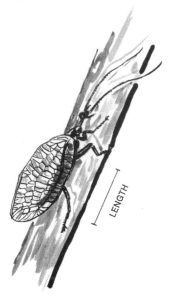

LENGTH

Lacewing.

an invertebrate, an animal without a backbone. All animals can be divided into two groups: vertebrate animals with backbones and internal skeletons, and invertebrate animals without backbones. Many invertebrate animals have segmented bodies. If you look at an earthworm or any insect, you can see lines on its body that divide it into sections. These sections are called segments.

Our green-and-gold creature has a segmented body. It also has jointed legs. Scientists call animals with segmented bodies and jointed legs Arthropoda, from the Greek words for "jointed" and "foot." This is the scientific name used all over the world for all animals without backbones, with segmented bodies, and jointed legs. When you say Arthropoda, you are speaking an international language.

All arthropods have outer coverings made of chitin, a tough material that does not stretch. This outer covering is known as the exoskeleton. As young arthropods feed, they grow inside their exoskeletons. Finally the exoskeleton tears down the back, and the animal crawls out. For a little while its new outer covering is soft and flexible. The animal stretches and makes space for new growth. Then the new exoskeleton becomes hard, and the arthropod will not get any bigger until it molts again.

All the animals in our imaginary collection were arthropods. They all had exoskeletons and jointed legs; but they did not have the same number of legs. Some had eight, some had six, and one had thirty. Animals with six legs are classed as Hexapoda (Greek again; *hex* means "six"). These are insects. Our little golden-eyed animal has six legs. It is an insect. It also has two pairs of wings. All insects with wings are adult. They will never get any bigger, and they are ready to reproduce.

The animal with soft green wings is a lacewing. When spring comes, she will lay her eggs on a leaf near an aphid (plant louse) colony. Her young will be ferocious-looking little black creatures called aphid lions. Aphid lions grab aphids in their pincer-like jaws and suck all their body juices. They rapidly eat their way through an aphid colony. Because lacewings are so useful in controlling aphids, they should be protected. If this were a real hunt instead of an imaginary one, the lacewing should be returned to the cool building.

You may be thinking that this is only an imaginary shelter, that the buildings near your house don't have these creatures. Maybe they haven't. No two shelters are exactly alike. But many small animals spend the winter in places like bandstands, sheds, garages, covered bridges, and barns. All of the invertebrates found in the imaginary building can sometimes be found in such shelters. So can house flies, cluster flies, blow flies, nests of mud-dauber wasps, ladybird beetles, plant bugs, and other kinds of cocoons, as well as a variety of other invertebrates. Just what is in the building will depend on its location, its construction, its floors, the part of the country where you live, and the things that affected the local environment that year, such as weather conditions and bird migrations, spray programs, a forest fire, or the cutting down of woods for a housing project or covering a field with asphalt to make a parking lot. This is why a record of the place and the date are important. If you are going to keep a permanent record, it should include the following:

Name of the animal

If you do not know the name, you can write a description. It is good to attach a drawing or photograph.

Stage of development

Egg, larva, pupa, adult, nymph, cocoon. Some animals always overwinter in the same stage. Some overwinter in different stages.

Address

The street and city or township or district.

Locality

For example: "In the crevice of bark on a red oak tree in Mr. Smith's farm woods"; or: "Under the window ledge of P. S. 56."

Date

Month, day, and year are important. Do not use numbers for the name of the month. 2/11/70 means February 11, 1970, to some people; to others, it means the second of November, 1970.

Activity

What was your insect doing? Did it move at all when you disturbed it?

Position

In what position were its legs, antennae, wings?

Neighbors

Was it with other creatures of the same kind? How many? Was it near creatures that differed from it? What kind? How near?

Any other observations

Unless you write things down, you forget—everyone does. If you keep careful records you can go back years later and make comparisons and draw conclusions.

CHAPTER *3*

Housing for Small Animals

Different people will enjoy making different studies with invertebrate animals in winter. You may just want to take an animal census to see how many different kinds of invertebrates you can find in different places. You may not want to bring anything indoors, or if you do, you may want to take notes and return the animals to their winter homes (except for mosquitoes and other problem insects). You may want to see more and to find answers to questions that occur to you as you look at your collection.

You may think that it would be fun to see those baby spiders hatch from their egg case. You may wonder what kind of webs they weave, or what color the moth is that is developing in those cocoons. There are many questions you will ask.

When will the lacewing wake up and start flying?

Does the woolly bear caterpillar have to eat some more before it spins a cocoon?

Do warm days make any difference in the behavior of these animals?

How soon will the moths emerge from their cocoons?

To find answers to these questions, it is necessary to make many observations. You could do this by going back to the same spot many times, but this might not be possible, and you might not always get the right answer.

Suppose your lacewing disappeared. Would you know if it crawled or flew away or was eaten by the centipede? Of course, there could be evidence—like bits of wings and legs—but even then, could you tell if the lacewing had been eaten by a centipede, or by a mouse or some other animal?

You might be able to make more frequent observations and have more control over what happens if you brought your animals indoors. But if you did that, you would be moving the creatures from winter to an artificial summer, and your conclusions would not be valid.

If you put the animals into containers and kept them in a cold place like a fire escape, a porch, or a

Vegetable crisper animal home.

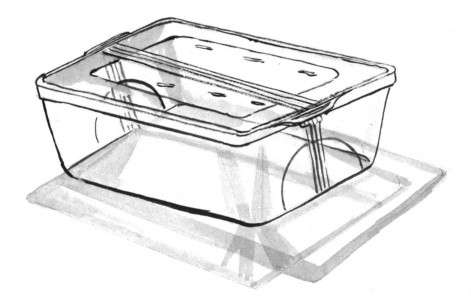

garage, you would be able to make daily observations that are still valid for the winter season. Then, when spring came, you could bring your animals indoors so you could watch them.

This has many advantages, for providing food for most animals can be a real problem in the wintertime. In addition, some animals, like the lacewing, which lay eggs as soon as spring comes, will not have the right places to lay them. Plastic vegetable crispers or any of the other small plastic boxes with lids can be made into good small animal homes.

As long as these are kept outdoors and the occupants are sleeping, there will be plenty of air. To provide more air, you can make windows by heating a knife and pressing it against the plastic. If you rotate your tool, you can make a round window. If you slide the knife blade back and forth, your window will be a narrow slit.

If you are keeping cocoons or pupae of large insects or animals, like big beetles, a row of small round windows just below the lid on each side of the crisper can be fine. But if you are keeping a variety of small animals or a piece of log that might have animals of different sizes in it, it will be much safer to make slit windows. Some tiny animals can even walk out of a slit window! For these very small creatures you may have to paste something like gauze over the windows.

You can also solve the oxygen problem by making your animal home into a terrarium. Put pebbles or gravel over the bottom. Add some charcoal to keep mold from forming. Add a layer of soil. Plant seeds; grass seed or bird seed will be fine. This will also provide some moisture for your little creatures. This is important, for insects are very sensitive to drying out. In fact, many moths and butterflies kept in a school-room never succeed in opening their wings because they have become so dried out that they do not have enough body fluid to expand their wings beyond the tiny size that they were in the pupa wing cases.

A house for nonflying insects may not need any windows or plants, since you can safely take the lid off to observe them and to add food. When you do this, there will be enough exchange of air to take care of the animals' oxygen needs for at least a day.

Just as different types of windows or nonwindows may be necessary for different animals, so different kinds of furnishing will be needed.

Some of the simplest and most interesting creatures to raise are caterpillars. If you find caterpillar eggs or woolly bear caterpillars, you should keep them outdoors until tree leaves begin to open. Then bring them indoors, where you can watch what happens. Caterpillars will do well in a container that has nothing in it but a small vial of water covered with a piece of cardboard or aluminum foil through which twigs of the food plant have been stuck. The cardboard or aluminum-foil cover keeps the caterpillar from crawling or falling into the water.

Keep records from the very beginning. You'll be surprised at how the young caterpillars grow and change. A good way to keep records is to draw the animal exactly as big as it is and put the date under it.

Examine the caterpillar's body. Insect bodies are divided into three sections. The part between the head and abdomen is called the thorax. Insect legs are attached to the thorax. Most caterpillars also have

Vial with parsley and swallowtail caterpillar.

fleshy leglike projections on their abdomens. These are called prolegs. How many prolegs have your caterpillars? Do they all have the same number? How do they use these structures? Let a caterpillar cling to your finger. How do the prolegs feel? Turn it over and look at a proleg with a hand lens. Are you surprised by what you see? Does this give you any ideas for an art project?

Caterpillar

Offer your caterpillars different kinds of foods. Do they always select the same food if they are given a choice? Keep a record of the number of leaves eaten each day. Make a graph of your figures. Does it climb steadily? Are there dips? If so, how many? Can you account for any irregularities?

Think of questions you can ask about the caterpillar. These could involve things like light, temperature, noise, food. Set up experiments to discover the answers.

Animals that normally live in houses can be kept indoors in winter. For instance, house crickets always live in buildings. Field crickets often move into houses when it gets cold. So if you find either house crickets or field crickets you can keep them as pets in the wintertime just as people do in Japan, China, and Korea. Crickets will eat bread, meat, vegetables. You can experiment to discover what they like best.

A female cricket has a long egg-laying organ called an ovipositor on the end of her body. She uses this to bury her eggs in the ground. Adult male crickets do the singing. If you have a male cricket, try to sneak up on him while he is singing and see how he makes his music.

If you have crickets, it is safer to put each one in a different house because crickets often kill each other. In fact, cricket fighting is a favorite sport in China. The owner of the champion fighter takes it from place to place to challenge other crickets, and people gather to watch the fight.

No matter what animals you rear or whether you are doing it all year or just in the spring and summer, you will need to keep your animal home clean. If it is a terrarium, the droppings will fall into the grass and become a part of the soil. If the home is a bare room for caterpillars with nothing but a vial of plant food, you can easily lift the caterpillar out on the leaves and shake the droppings out. Usually this will be all that is necessary; but if the floor of your animal house gets dirty, it can be easily washed with mild soap and water, then rinsed and dried.

Plastic-crisper and hatbox homes are not the only kinds of insect houses you can make. You can use your imagination in creating homes with boxes of cardboard or clear plastic, or in jars, or from wire screening. The important thing is to provide your animals with the things they need to be healthy, in a home where you can observe their behavior and growth.

Sometimes you may find animals you can't identify. The key to invertebrate animals in the appendix will help you decide what you have.

CHAPTER *4*

Wooden Dormitories

A dead log is a good place from which to collect in-vertebrate animals. You can find dead logs in parks and woods, along a railroad track, in a fence cor-ner, or on a vacant city lot. Often logs may be found on uncultivated land along a stream or river. Part of a fallen tree, an abandoned railroad tie, or even an old piece of board will harbor interesting life.

Many creatures use dead wood for food and shel-ter. Most of the time these creatures are very useful. Try to imagine what the world would look like to-day if all the plants and animals that have lived on earth in the last billion years had not been eaten by other animals or destroyed by bacteria after they died. Not only would there be no space to stand, but all the raw materials like oxygen, carbon, nitro-gen, calcium, iron, and sulfur would be used up.

Because we do not like the things in our homes to decay or be eaten by insects, we often forget that these processes are very important to us. So, when termites get into houses and eat the dead wood from which the houses are made, we say that termites are destruc-tive, bad animals. What we should understand is that termites are destructive when they move in with peo-

⊢────⊣
LENGTH

Termite in winter nest.

31

ple, but outdoors, in the woods, termites are useful creatures—part of the great interrelated circle of life.

If you are lucky, you may find termites hibernating in a log. In fact, a log is often like a dormitory. Some animals that live in it all year will be sleeping there. So may creatures that lived nearby and moved into the spaces in the log that were hollowed out by different animals during the summer months. Some of these spaces are like small rooms; others are narrow hallways called galleries that connect one room with another in ant and termite colonies.

Termites that live in logs in warm months often move deep into the earth when the weather turns cold, but if their log home is thick, some of the workers may hibernate in the galleries in the center. Often, large numbers of worker termites will be piled on top of each other, so that the galleries are tightly packed. Ice crystals form on their bodies and decorate the gallery walls and ceiling.

Sometimes large numbers of ants may also be found in their summer galleries in a log. Their legs interlock, so if you pick up one, you may be holding

Carpenter ants in their sawdust nests.

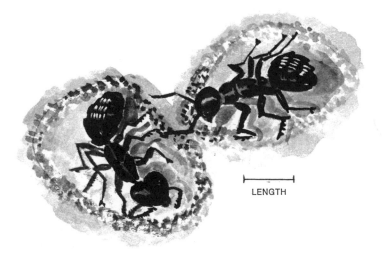

LENGTH

LENGTH

Ladybird beetles congregating.

a chain or ball of ants. Ice crystals also form around them. Sometimes a big carpenter ant may make a room for itself under the bark of a log by making walls of sawdust.

Spiders also are often found between the bark and the log. Spiders sleep under a closely woven silken blanket. After you have looked under a number of spider blankets, you will begin to realize that different kinds of spiders overwinter at different ages. Notice the position of the spiders' legs while they are hibernating. Is there any difference between spiders of different ages in this respect?

Sometimes large numbers of ladybird beetles can be found under the bark in a cavity in the log. If the space is large enough, ladybird beetles may gather in hundreds or even thousands.

Red ladybird beetles with black trim eat aphids; all-black ladybird beetles and black ones with red marks usually eat scale insects. These beetles are so

LENGTH

Black ladybird beetle.

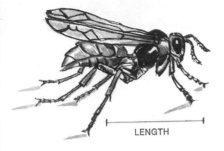

LENGTH

Polistes wasp.

LENGTH

Bumblebee queen.

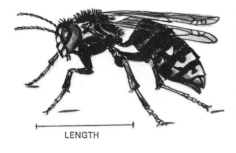

LENGTH

White-faced hornet queen.

useful that some kinds of them are gathered in their winter dormitories high in the Rocky Mountains and kept in cold storage until spring, when they are sold to gardeners and orchardists, who are happy to have these small animals work for them.

Sometimes a dozen or two queen wasps will be found piled on top of each other. In the spring each of these will make a nest of paper cells. The nest will be one flat platform. It will not have a paper bag around it like a hornet's nest. These wasps are called *Polistes* wasps, a name taken from a Greek word that means "founder of a city." Some observation will disclose why this is a good name for this insect.

Other queens also hide in logs, but they hide singly instead of in groups. If you are fortunate, you may find a fat bumblebee queen with her black-and-gold velvet body. Or you may find a white-faced hornet queen with her wings held close to her sides by her hind legs, asleep in the little room she chewed out of dead wood for herself before it became cold.

Most of the invertebrate animals discussed so far have moved into the log dormitory for the winter. Only two are sleeping in their summer galleries.

Most beetles found in logs live there summer and winter. Adult beetles are usually easy insects to recognize. They generally have hard, shiny wing covers, under which their gauzy wings are folded. When a beetle flies, it opens the covers like a pair of doors and holds them out at the side. Only the gauzy underneath wings are used in flying.

Beetles belong to the kinds of insects whose young do not look at all like the adult. There are many different kinds of beetles and many kinds of beetle larvae. Click beetles are one kind of beetle found in logs. Have you ever caught a click beetle in the summer and laid him on his back and watched him flip himself into the air until he landed on his feet and could run away?

Click beetles come in brown, black, and gray tones. Most of them are small—from an eighth of an inch to a half inch in length. A few are about an inch long, and the most handsome one of the group is two inches long. This big fellow is different from his relatives in a number of ways. He is gray and has two big black dots on his thorax.

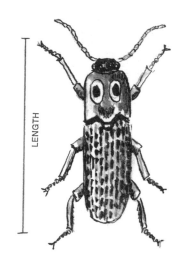

The black dots have white edges, which make them look like eyes. Because of this, this beetle is called the eyed-click-beetle, or eyed-elator. Of course these aren't real eyes. They are just decorations. As with all other insects, this beetle's eyes are on its head. It takes the eyed-click-beetle three years to grow from an egg to an adult, so one- and two-year-old eyed-click-beetles may also be found in the log. Click-beetle larvae are smooth, hard, orange-brown, and shiny. Except for their antennae and the six short legs, they look much like worms. In fact, they are often called wireworms. Only experts who specialize in click beetles can tell one wireworm from another. However, if you find a wireworm that is over an inch long in a log, you can almost be sure that you have a two-year-old eyed-click-beetle.

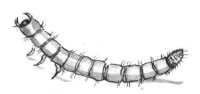

Eyed-click-beetle and larva.

If you find an eyed-click-beetle in a log, it is probably hibernating in its home. Eyed-click-beetles and their larvae live on other insects. A dead log may be a fine dining room for them. Some other click beetles feed on dead wood. They are also all-year residents of logs. Many of them mature in one year and spend

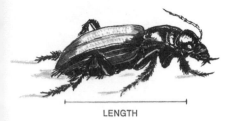

LENGTH

Tiger beetle.

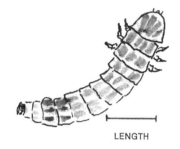

LENGTH

Firefly larva.

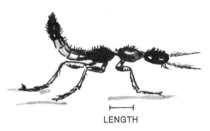

LENGTH

Rove beetle.

the winter as pupae in little cells they have dug out of the wood.

Tiger beetles and fireflies also feed on other invertebrate animals. Tiger beetles spend the winter as adults. They are handsome creatures with metallic green, black, or brown wing covers with yellow stripes or dots. In summer they can run fast on their slender black legs. Their strong jaws grab their prey.

Fireflies are another kind of beetle. Their wing covers are not as hard or shiny as the wing covers of tiger beetles or ladybird beetles. They overwinter in the larval stage. Many firefly larvae give off light in the same way adult fireflies do. If you find a flat, wingless creature with six short legs and a pale spot that glows in the dark on the underside of its abdomen, you have found a young firefly. Some firefly larvae do not emit light, but they are shaped just like the larvae that do.

Rove beetles may also be found in the log. They have short wing covers that leave seven or eight segments of their abdomen exposed. Most of them have strong gauzy wings folded under their wing covers just like other beetles. A few have no wings and cannot fly.

There are thousands of kinds of rove beetles. They range in size from less than an eighth of an inch to an inch in length. They are brown, black, or gray. Sometimes they have bright-red or orange wing covers, and often the wing covers have stripes and spots of bright colors. Sometimes there are tufts of colored hairs on their abdomens. Most rove beetles eat other invertebrates. Some kinds live on ants and are found near ant colonies.

Once in a while, a butterfly may be found hibernating in a log. Most butterflies overwinter as pupae, but some spend the winter as larvae, some as eggs, and one family, the angle wings, spend the winter as adult butterflies. Angle wings get their name from their angled and notched front wings. Often the hind wings are notched, too. The red admiral, the painted lady, and the mourning cloak are the three best-known members of the family.

WING SPREAD 3"

Mourning cloak butterfly.

The red admiral is a handsome black butterfly with white dots and diagonal red stripes across the fore wings and a red border on the hind wings.

The painted lady is blotched and spotted. It is a soft orangey-tan color with dark-brown markings, white spots, and blotches of salmon pink.

The mourning cloak is a rich brown color. It has a wide gold border on its fore and hind wings. Just inside the border is a row of pale-blue dots.

The wings of the red admiral and the mourning cloak are dull brown and black on the underside. When these butterflies rest with their wings closed, they look like dead leaves. The painted lady is "painted" on its undersurface as well as on the top surface. Even so, with closed wings it looks a lot like an autumn leaf that still has some red color. You must be very observant in order to locate these lovely creatures in their winter quarters, since they always sleep with their wings closed.

Insects are not the only invertebrate animals that overwinter in logs. As you examine the log, you may find a silvery trail laid down by a snail or slug as it prepared for winter. If you follow the trail, you may find that it leads to a large patch of dried mucus. Behind this, in a little cell that it chewed out of the wood, a slug is curled up. If you use your knife to dig

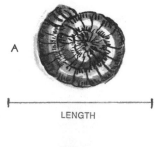

A

LENGTH

B

LENGTH

C

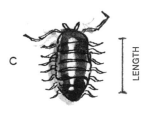

LENGTH

(A) Millipede. (B) Pillbug.
(C) Sowbug.

it out, you will discover that the slug is entirely enclosed in dried mucus, which it secreted before it went to sleep. Snails usually hide beneath stones or logs for the winter. They secrete a mucus plug that closes the opening of their shells and protects their soft bodies.

Millipedes may also be found curled up in a wooden cell that they have chewed out of the wood. The word millipede means "thousand feet." This is an exaggeration. Millipedes have two pairs of legs on almost every segment of their bodies. Different kinds of millipedes have different numbers of body segments. You can get an approximate count of a millipede's legs by counting the segments of its body and multiplying this number by four. Since all millipedes have at least thirty segments, any millipede will have over a hundred legs.

Other invertebrates that are sometimes found in or under logs are sowbugs and pillbugs. These are crustaceans and are related to shrimps, crayfish, and lobsters. They are unusual because all their relatives live in water. Their breathing apparatus is much like the gills of their aquatic relatives. Therefore they must always live in moist places. Like their relatives, they have two pairs of antennae. The long pair is very conspicuous. In the winter the sowbug lies flat, with its antennae and its legs pointing backward. The pillbug curls up in a ball. Its legs and soft parts are protected. Full-grown pillbugs and sowbugs are about one-half inch long. When the weather gets warm, the waving antennae of pillbugs and sowbugs are one of the first signs that they are waking up.

There is a great difference in the ways in which animals sleep through the winter. Many are truly hibernating. All their body activities have slowed down, and nothing disturbs them or wakens them. Others seem to be napping. They waken on warm days. Like baby spiders and the lacewing in our imaginary building, they may move their legs and antennae.

If any of the little animals you find are active, be sure to put this fact in your record. You may be able to add to scientific knowledge, for there is still much that we do not know about the winter behavior of many invertebrate animals.

CHAPTER 5

An Egg Hunt

Sometimes you may want to hunt for a lot of examples of a particular thing. Instead of going to one place, like a building or a log, you will need to go to many places. Winter can be a fine time for an egg hunt.

Your hand lens will be very useful, for the eggs you will be finding will be small. In fact, you will probably want to collect specimens and take them indoors where you can examine them in comfort. A brown paper bag will make a fine egg basket into which you can drop twigs, leaves, and other larger objects on which you find eggs. You will also want some small bags or vials, so individual eggs or small specimens do not get lost in your egg basket. A knife will be useful for cutting twigs and lifting specimens from crannies, or you may want to take pruning shears or kitchen scissors for cutting twigs so the bark does not get torn and damaged.

You can be almost sure of finding eggs if you can find a wild cherry tree. If you live in the country, this will not be hard, for they grow along fences and roads in many places. In the city you may find them in a vacant lot or along a railroad track. Try to

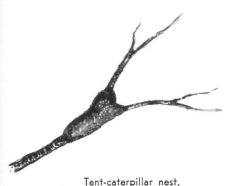

Tent-caterpillar nest.

remember where you saw tent-caterpillar nests last spring. They probably were on wild cherry trees. Even if they weren't, any tree that had a tent caterpillar nest on it is a good place to start your egg hunt.

Look at the tips of the branches. One or more of them will probably have a grayish tube-shaped structure near the tip that looks as though it had been slipped over the twig and pushed down until it stuck. Even without a hand lens you can see a hundred to two hundred or more little gray spheres glued together and covered with a protective coating that looks like varnish.

These are eggs of the common tent caterpillar. They were laid in late summer by a reddish-brown moth. During the summer and fall, little caterpillars developed inside the eggs but did not hatch. Instead, they remained curled up in their tiny shells, ready to emerge in spring to build houses of silk and to eat the fresh, tender green leaves of the cherry tree.

Each moth lays all of her eggs in one cluster, but several moths may lay their eggs on one tree. Some years it is easy to gather thousands of eggs in a very little space.

Fortunately, these eggs make good food for some birds. They are the chickadees' idea of a fine scrambled-egg breakfast. In fact, chickadees and nuthatches provide good clues for egg hunting.

The common tent caterpillar also lays its eggs on apple, plum, and other fruit trees. Other kinds of tent caterpillars lay their eggs on forest trees and shrubs.

If you are fortunate and look carefully, you may find "baskets" full of eggs hanging on the ends of branches of many different kinds of trees. These bas-

kets or bags were made by the caterpillars of the
bagworm moth. Often the bags hang over city streets
and sidewalks, and hundreds and thousands of people walk past them without realizing that they are
overhead. If they look up and see the bags, they may
think they are dead leaves still hanging on the tree.
This is not surprising because the egg baskets are well
camouflaged. Early in the spring, when leaves begin
to open on the trees, young bagworm caterpillars
hatch and make silk bags that entirely cover their
bodies except for a small opening at the rear and
a large opening through which their heads and legs
extend in the front. They attach small twigs, leaves,
grains of sand, or lichens to the bag. Each time they
molt they make their bag bigger and attach more
material.

Bagworm cocoon.

There are twenty kinds of bagworms in the United
States, and each kind makes its own style of dress.
Some fasten the twigs crosswise; others fasten them
lengthwise. Some are as small as one third of an inch
long when they are ready to pupate; others are more
than two inches long. Their bags protect them from
enemies. In fact, if they are scared, they pull their
heads into the bag and sit still, and only an enemy
with very sharp eyes can tell them from leaves or
a piece of bark.

When it is time to pupate, they fasten the bag to
a twig, close both ends, and have a ready-made
cocoon.

Until this time, the male and female have developed in the same way, but now something very surprising happens. Inside the cocoon the male develops
wings, feathery antennae, and slender legs, just like
any other moth. But the female doesn't develop any

of these things. Instead, she loses her legs. Some kinds of bagworm females lose their eyes and mouths, too. Changes are taking place inside her body also. Her digestive tract disappears. Her whole body fills up with eggs. When she emerges from her pupal skin, she stays in the cocoon. She wiggles down to the bottom and makes a hole in the bag and waits for a mate.

When the male is ready to emerge as a moth, the pupa pushes its way partly out of the bottom of the cocoon. Then the pupal skin breaks. The moth crawls out of this skin, stretches, dries his wings, and flies away to find a female to mate with.

After she mates, the female lays her eggs in the bag. Soon the bag is filled with eggs. In some kinds of bagworms, the female's shriveled body remains in the bag. In others, she crawls out the hole in the bottom of the bag, drops to the ground, and dies.

In the winter, bags built by females will contain two hundred or more yellow eggs. A case built by a male will have the dried pupa case hanging out the bottom if the wind has not blown it away.

Some people in India who believe in reincarnation say that thieves turn into bagworms when they die and have to carry all the things they stole in their lifetime as humans in the form of dried leaves and twigs.

If you find scale insects, you might have another abundant supply of eggs. The story of scale insects is similar to the bagworm story. Scale insects are tiny creatures that make a wax "roof" called a scale. The scale may be shaped like an oyster shell or a mussel shell, or it may be pear-shaped, round, or oval. Often the male insect makes a scale that is a

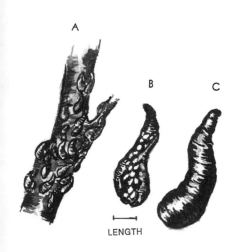

A

B   C

LENGTH

Oyster-shell scales: (A) Branch female scales. (B) Female turned over to show eggs. (C) Female.

different shape from the female's. The males' scales are always smaller than the females'.

The wax scale is fastened to a young branch, a leaf, or a fruit. As soon as it starts to make a scale, the insect molts for the first time. It loses its eyes and legs. Now it cannot move around. It is just a little round, soft-bodied creature with a big appetite. It has a sharp, piercing, sucking mouth that pumps sap and plant juices into its stomach. It cannot move away from enemies, but it is well protected from them and from the weather by its wax roof.

When it is almost grown, the male scale insect pupates. This is very unusual. None of the other insects with piercing, sucking mouthparts pupate; they all have gradual metamorphosis.

The female scale insect behaves like her relatives —she does not pupate. She goes on feeding while the male pupates; then she molts for the last time. Except that she is bigger, she looks just the same as she did after her first molt. She is an eyeless, legless grub. But she is not exactly the same, for now her body is full of eggs.

Two common scale insects are the oyster-shell scale and the pine-needle scale. The oyster-shell scale can be found on many different kinds of trees and bushes. It is curved like an oyster shell and is a dirty brown-and-gray color that blends very well with the tree bark. Sometimes the scales are so close together that they look like the interlocking pieces of a jigsaw puzzle. Each scale is about an eighth of an inch long when fully grown.

The pine-needle scale looks more like a tiny mussel than an oyster shell. The scale is white. A half dozen or more may be lined up on each needle, so

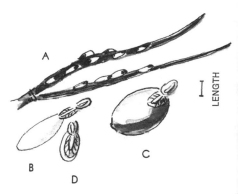

Pine-needle scales: (A) Infested pine needles. (B) and (C) Two kinds of female scales. (D) Male scale.

that the tree looks as if it were covered with a light sprinkling of snow.

Both of these insects lay eggs in the fall. There may be anywhere from fifteen to a hundred white eggs under the scale of an oyster-shell scale, and about twenty to thirty-five purple eggs under that of the pine-needle scale. In addition to white and purple eggs, scale insects lay yellow and orange eggs. The dried-up body of the mother will always be found with the eggs. The scales that were made by the males will be empty except for the pupal skin.

Some kinds of scale insects never lay eggs. Instead, the female holds the eggs in her body until they hatch. Scales of this type will have half-grown male and female scale insects beneath them in winter.

You will need your hand lens to examine the scales and count scale-insect eggs.

Not all eggs are laid on trees. You will find that bushes and weeds are good collecting places. An interesting egg case, which is found on weeds or low bushes, is made by the praying mantis. This egg case looks as though it were made of baked meringue. In the fall the females build the cases from a transparent

Mantis cases: Carolina, European, and Chinese.

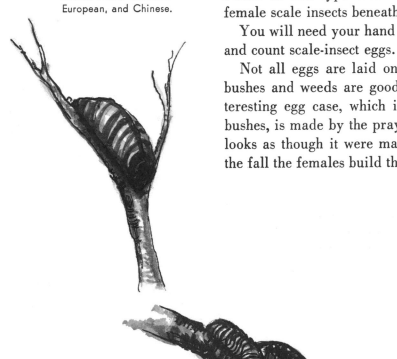

substance that looks much like egg white. As this escapes from their bodies, they beat air into it, then stick their tail into the froth and lay eggs in it. The eggs are arranged in layers. Each layer has a weak spot along the edge. All the weak spots are one above the other, so they form a band down the center of the egg case. When the young hatch, they escape through this band.

The egg case of the Chinese mantis is almost as great in diameter as it is long, and it has a flat top. The native American mantises, which live in the southern United States, and the European mantises make long, narrow egg cases with rounded ends. Mantis egg cases often contain over two hundred eggs.

The garden spider also hangs her egg cocoon on bushes and weeds. This is made of silk. In the fall, the female spins a heavy square of silk, in which she lays a hundred or more eggs. Then she pulls the corners together and fastens them to make a silky bag. She carries this bag up a tree and fixes it to a branch with some more silk.

Banded-garden-spider egg case.

The young spiders soon hatch, but they stay inside the cocoon. Since no insects are in their silk house, they eat each other when they get hungry. In cold weather they are inactive, but on warm winter days they wake up and eat. By spring, only a small number of young spiders are left in the silk cocoon.

Not all invertebrate animals lay their eggs in one mass. Some lay them in several small masses, and others scatter them one by one.

Walking sticks walk along the branches of trees and drop their eggs to the ground one at a time in the fall of the year. Sometimes so many walking sticks are

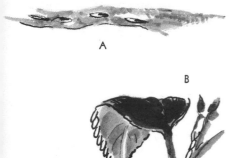

(A) Northern katydid slits in twig for eggs. (B) Angular-winged-katydid eggs on leaf and twig.

laying eggs in the same section of the woods that it sounds like rain falling.

Dragonflies scatter their eggs over the pond bottom by flying in circles over the pond and dropping one egg at a time into the water.

Grasshoppers bury several packets of eggs in holes that they dig in the ground with the rear of their abdomens.

Some kinds of katydids put several rows of eggs in slits that they make in small branches. Others lay them on the edges of leaves. You may find a twig with a row of small slits in the bark, or a leaf on the ground with a neat row of eggs on the edge of the underside.

All eggs that are scattered or buried are hard to find. Many of them are hard to identify.

You might want to preserve a few of your eggs in jars of alcohol. If you do this, you should make careful notes of the colors before you put them in the jar, for the alcohol will fade them or turn them brown. Of course you must make notes on the date and the place where you made your collection.

If you want to know more about the little animals that will hatch from the eggs you can put the eggs in your observation cage outdoors. Many eggs need the cold weather to make them hatch. Even eggs that do not need the cold often dry out and die in warm houses, or they hatch so early that there is no food for them, so they starve to death.

When spring comes, it is a good idea to move the eggs indoors to terraria or glass jars with moist earth in the bottom and cheesecloth over the top. There, emerging insects can be fed and watched. If you have a lot of young praying mantises or spiders, you should release some of them so they can grow up and help harvest some of the extra insects that feed in gardens. If you have a lot of bagworm egg baskets or tent-caterpillar egg masses, tree owners and chickadees would both be happy if you put them in a bird-feeding station.

CHAPTER 6

Chickadee Punching Bags and Squirrel Desserts

If you ever see a chickadee vigorously pecking a gray object that hangs on, or near, the end of a wild cherry or lilac branch and swings back and forth with each blow like a miniature punching bag, you will be well rewarded if you take time to investigate.

At first the object may seem like a twisted gray leaf. This is not surprising, for the outer covering was made from a leaf by the two-inch-long bluish-green caterpillar of the Promethea moth, which had fed on the tree throughout the summer. When fall came and the big Promethea caterpillar with its six short yellow legs and its double row of red, yellow, and black knobs called tubercles was ready to pupate, it used silk to fasten the petiole (the stem) of a leaf firmly to the branch. Then it coated the leaf's upper surface with a gummy substance and covered it with silk. As the caterpillar worked, it used bands of silk to draw the edges of the leaf together, so that the leaf

Promethea cocoon.

formed a cylinder that enclosed and hid it from view.

Inside this cylinder, the caterpillar continued to spin until it had made a firm, tough case, in which it shed its skin and turned into a dark-brown pupa.

At first glance this pupa does not look at all like the beautiful moth it is going to become. But if you look closely, you will find that the surface is sculptured with the body segments, the wings, the eyes, and the antennae.

In fact, the sculpturing is so complete that you can tell by looking at the antennae whether this will be a male or a female moth. The antennae of male Promethea moths are broad and feathery; those of the female are much narrower.

When the moth emerges in the spring, other characteristics will also indicate its sex. Female moths have fat bodies, filled with eggs, while the bodies of the males are smaller and much more slender. In addition, male Promethea moths are a different color than the females. The male's wings are very dark, sometimes a maroon brown, sometimes chocolate brown, sometimes almost black, with deep cream-colored or light-brown edges. The female's wings are light brown, and the light edges are two-toned, with interesting dots and squiggles.

The males fly in the daytime, and the females fly only at night. The females give off an odor that the males smell with special organs in their broad antennae. The male Promethea moth's sense of smell for the female Promethea moth's perfume is so good that he sometimes flies for more than a mile to join a female. If you have a female Promethea moth, you can usually attract male Prometheas if you tie thread gently around the female's body and attach her to something in the yard, or in the house on the inside of a screen door or screened window. The latter is a better place if you are not going to watch her every minute, because a bird or even a squirrel may snatch the captive prize for its dinner when you are not looking if it is anchored outside.

Sometimes the "chickadee punching bag" is larger and broader than the Promethea cocoon and the outline of the leaf more marked. This is a cocoon of the Cynthia moth. You may find Cynthia cocoons on lilac and wild cherry or other trees on which Promethea live, but the favorite food of the Cynthia caterpillar is the leaf of the ailanthus tree. Cynthia caterpillars fed on ailanthus leaves in China long before the animals were brought to the United States in 1861. Cynthias were imported to this country because it was hoped that silk thread and cloth could be made from the cocoons.

When this proved impractical, some of the moths were released. There were plenty of ailanthus trees on which they could lay eggs because ailanthus trees had been brought to the United States in 1784; since these trees are rapid growers, produce many wind-carried seeds, and grow well in cities as well as rural areas, they could be found almost everywhere by 1861. In places that lacked ailanthus trees the moths found other trees that Cynthia caterpillars enjoyed. Soon the lovely tan-and-pink Cynthia moths were as common here as the native American silk moths to which they are related: the Promethea, Cecropia, Polyphemus, and Luna moths.

You will find Cecropia cocoons fastened to a twig, a board, or some other flat surface. They never contain leaves, nor are they fastened to a leaf. They never

Cecropia cocoon.

hang down below a branch. They are three or four inches long and about an inch and a half high at the thickest part. They vary in color from a pale tan to gray, brown, and almost red. The outer covering is peaked and angled. Inside, a tightly woven second cocoon with rounded ends protects the pupa. Even so, birds with strong beaks, like bluejays and woodpeckers, sometimes succeed in tearing the cocoon open.

Mice and squirrels also enjoy moth pupae when they can reach them, and of course these cocoons are easier to reach and feed on than the tough swinging ones of the Promethea and Cynthia moths.

Parasitic wasps also lay eggs in the larvae and pupae of moths, so some cocoons will never develop into moths. In spite of these natural enemies, Cecropia moths used to be very common.

It was possible to collect them by the basketful. In one school, the students used a needle and thread to string hundreds of cocoons in long festoons, which they hung on the walls and crisscrossed across the room. One winter day when the children came to school, charts, desks, walls, and blackboard edges were covered with hundreds of beautiful reddish-brown moths with red, black, and white markings. Soon the females laid thousands of eggs all over the classroom. Unfortunately, the caterpillars that hatched from the eggs had no food and died.

Because so many Cecropia cocoons have been gathered in this way, the moths have become rare in many places. This is unfortunate because they are very beautiful, and the caterpillars seldom occur in large enough numbers to do any real damage.

Today, airplane spraying for gypsy moths and city spraying for flies and mosquitoes have also killed many of the big moths; so it is important to put any cocoons that you collect in a cold place until spring arrives and to release the moths after they emerge, so that these big moths will not die out and we will continue to see and enjoy them.

Polyphemus and Luna cocoons are more difficult to find than the Cecropia, Promethea, and Cynthia. Both make oval cocoons with leaves on the surface. The leaf enclosing the Polyphemus cocoon sometimes stays on the tree all winter, but usually it falls to the ground. The Luna cocoon always falls to the ground.

Even though the cocoons are the same size and shape, it is easy to tell a Luna from a Polyphemus cocoon. The Luna uses very little silk, and the cocoon is thin and feels soft. The Polyphemus spins a strong silken cocoon that feels tough if you gently squeeze it.

Polyphemus and Luna cocoons both contain pupae that are developing into handsome moths. The Polyphemus moth is a lovely tan creature with yellow, black, and blue markings. The Luna moth is a delicate pale green. It has a white body and purple legs, a purple edge on the fore wings, and long, slender green tails on the hind wings.

Many people think the Luna is the most beautiful North American moth. Certainly it is extremely beautiful, but there is such a wonderful variety of form and color that there are beauties to suit every taste. Selecting only one moth as the most beautiful would be very difficult.

Many other smaller moths overwinter in cocoons. The cocoons that we found in the imaginary garage had the hairs from the caterpillar mixed in with the silk of the cocoon. They were probably made by the

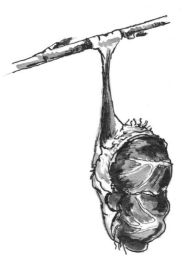

Polyphemus cocoon.

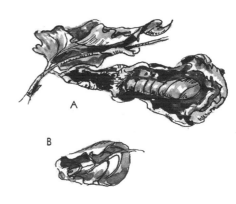

(A) Luna cocoon cut open to show pupa. (B) Closed cocoon.

yellow woolly bear caterpillar and contained a pupa that was developing into an acrea moth with a yellow abdomen, a white thorax, and white fore wings. The female acrea moth has white hind wings; the male's hind wings are yellow. Both males and females have black spots on their wings and bodies.

This kind of moth is very common. However, if you collect cocoons of this type you may have a surprise, for the acrea moth has many relatives that use their caterpillar hairs as part of their cocoon. Some moth caterpillars make very thin cocoons from a small amount of silk. You often can see the dark pupa between the threads. Cocoons of this type are found under pieces of board, beneath loose bark on tree trunks, and in other sheltered spots.

Cocoons vary in size from the big Cecropia cocoon to the tiny ones made by small caterpillars that spend their whole lives between the upper and lower layers of a leaf and feed on the chlorophyll. You need a hand lens to examine these cocoons and the tiny moths that emerge from them.

Not all moths make cocoons. Generally, moth caterpillars that form naked pupae enter the ground and dig out little cells for themselves. They pupate in these small underground chambers, where they are safe from birds and many other enemies. In fact, after the ground freezes, practically nothing can disturb them except a bulldozer or a backhoe or a very sharp pick swung by a boy with strong muscles. It is much easier to collect the pupae of moths of this type in the fall, before cold weather arrives.

Frequently you can gather large moth pupae in an area that is being plowed or spaded in the fall. Gardens that had tomato and potato plants, or fields of potatoes or tobacco, are especially good places to search.

If you are fortunate, you will find a large brown pupa with what looks like a slender curved handle. The "handle" contains the proboscis of the moth, a long, slender tonguelike mouthpart that enables the moth to feed on the nectar at the bottom of trumpet-shaped flowers.

Pupa of sphinx caterpillar.

These are pupae of sphinx caterpillars. Not all sphinx pupae have the special sheath for the proboscis, but any pupae that you find with this kind of a structure is a sphinx.

Sphinx caterpillars get their name from their habit of raising the front part of their bodies and contracting the head and thorax region so they looked like the legendary sphinx.

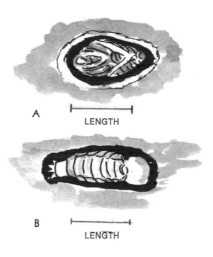

(A) Japanese-beetle pupa.
(B) Click-beetle pupa.

There are many kinds of sphinx moths. Some are gray; others have gray bodies and fore wings and colored hind wings; others are brown. Many have red, yellow, pink, or orange markings. All have long, narrow fore wings, short hind wings, and slender bodies. Some have a wingspread of as much as six inches; others have a wingspread of less than an inch.

Sphinx pupae are not the only moth pupae that are found buried in the earth. Telling one kind of naked pupa from another is very difficult. The best thing to do is to put the pupae in earth in a cage in a cool place and wait to see what emerges.

You may also find pupae of other insects with complete metamorphosis while you are collecting. Many beetle pupae are found in the earth. If you examine the sculptured organs on the outside, you

June-beetle pupa.

will discover some differences. Beetle pupae usually have pointed abdomens. Moths' abdomens are more rounded.

Many butterflies also overwinter in the pupal stage. You may find them hanging in some sheltered spot. Some kinds of butterfly caterpillars spin a little pad of silk. They attach the tail end of their body to the pad until they free their body from its old silk. Then the pupa grabs the silk pad with a special hook on the end of the abdomen. This is a tricky acrobatic feat. The pupa hangs head downward. Other caterpillars make both a silk pad and a silk sling. The abdomen hooks in the pad and the thorax rests against the sling. This pupa has its head pointing upward.

Butterfly pupae are called chrysalis. This comes from a Greek word meaning "gold." A few chrysalises are decorated with gold dots, but the ones that are found in winter are brown, tan, or gray. You will have to be very alert to find them.

Promethea and Cynthia have a special valve which they push open to escape from the cocoon; all other moths secrete a substance that wets the silk and helps the moth break and tear a path to the outside. Pupa cases and chrysalis cases are split open when moths and butterflies emerge. Often they are so fragile that they are easily broken.

A series of color changes often announces that the adult developing in the pupal skin is ready to emerge. This is a good time to bring your specimens in from their cool storage place and keep a close watch, so you will not miss one of the most exciting events of the insect world.

(A) Sling-type chrysalis of common sulphur butterfly. (B) Hanging-type chrysalis of pearl-crescent butterfly.

CHAPTER 7

Witches'-Brooms and Gingerbread Houses

The dark silhouette of witches'-brooms may be seen against the full moon in almost any part of the United States—of course, they can be seen on sunny days and gray days or by the light of a flashlight or street

Witches'-brooms by the light of the moon.

Goldenrod ball gall, cut open to show grub.

Goldenrod spindle gall, with ball gall above.

light, too! And gingerbreadlike houses may be found in any spot where green plants grow.

If you remember the story of the gingerbread house you know that it was a beautiful little house that provided a snug warm place as well as being good to eat.

There are thousands of kinds of houses just like this, which provide snug homes and food for invertebrate animal "children." These edible homes are called galls. A patch of goldenrod is a good place to become acquainted with galls.

Goldenrod grows along city streets and country roads, in the woods, in parks, along railroad tracks, in vacant lots. There are many different kinds of goldenrod, and all produce galls.

The four most common galls on goldenrod are called goldenrod ball gall, goldenrod spindle gall, goldenrod tapered-stem gall, and goldenrod bunch gall. All of these are easy to find in the winter, when leaves have fallen.

Goldenrod ball gall is a spherical swelling on the stem of a goldenrod plant. If you cut this gall in half lengthwise, you will find that the inside is made of a white, pithy material with an oval cell in the middle. Inside this cell is a fat white grub.

Sometimes the swelling is long and narrow—elliptical, instead of being round. This is a spindle gall. If you cut this gall in half lengthwise, you will find that it is hollow inside. In some parts of the country, a small moth may be spending the winter inside this hollow space. In other spindle galls, the empty pupal skin will show that an insect once lived there, and an open tunnel will show where the little moth escaped to find a spot to hibernate outside the gall.

If you are fortunate enough to find a gall with a moth in it, you will also be able to see the tunnel running to the outer layer of the goldenrod stem, for the moth caterpillar eats a tunnel almost to the surface of the gall before it pupates. Then, when it emerges as a moth without chewing mouthparts, it can escape just by pushing its head against the thin doorway.

The tapered-stem gall looks like the spindle gall but is smaller and located higher on the stem. Depending on the climate, it will contain either a caterpillar or a pupa during the winter months.

The fourth common goldenrod gall is called a bunch gall. It is formed when the stalk fails to elongate and all the leaves unfold close together. In the center of this leaf cluster is a single tough cell, which is generally empty in the winter time.

Scientists through the ages have been asking questions about galls. Some of their questions are probably the same ones you are thinking about.

What made the gall grow?

How did the insect get inside it?

Why are the galls different shapes?

Why do different galls contain different creatures?

Because people have been asking questions and searching for answers through careful observation and experiments, and have written down their discoveries for others to share, we have gradually collected some of the answers to these questions. For instance, we know that a caterpillar and a pupa and a moth are three different stages in the life of one creature; and if we open galls at different seasons and find caterpillars in winter or spring, pupae in summer, and moths in fall, we understand that these

Goldenrod bunch gall.

are different stages of the same kind of insect. But before men learned about insect metamorphosis, the variety of creatures in one kind of gall must have been very confusing. And if they inspected different galls and found still other things in them, they were even more puzzled.

Long ago, when people didn't understand things, they usually explained them as magic. They thought that magic affected their lives, so they used galls to tell fortunes. People who wanted to know about the future would go to someone they called a witch, or a magician, or a soothsayer, or a fortune-teller. Sometimes the person looking into the future would cut a gall open and would predict what was going to happen by examining the creature in the gall. It is interesting to imagine some of the predictions that would be made, based on whether the gall contained a single big, fat larva, or dozens of tiny larvae, or a sleeping pupa, or a fly, or a moth, or a tiny eight-legged creature called a mite, or a big family of aphids, or was completely empty. Any of these things could be found, depending on the kind of gall and the season of the year. Today we are still asking gall questions.

Perhaps the most often asked questions are about the way in which galls form. We know that some galls grow in response to a chemical that the mother insect puts on the plant when she lays an egg. Scientists have even made galls form on some plants by extracting body juices from adult gall insects and inoculating the plant. Other plants require baby insects to feed on them before they grow a gall. These two discoveries raise many more questions.

Galls are plant tumors. Some scientists think that

if they can obtain more answers to gall growth, they may find one of the keys to tumors and even to cancer in animals and people.

After you have become acquainted with some galls, you may want to set up your own research project so that you can make firsthand observations. You may even be able to add to scientific knowledge, for there are many gall-insect life histories that have never been completely worked out, and there are often other insects besides the original inhabitants in the gall. Some of these other insects, like some gall insects, have neither been studied nor even given a scientific name.

As a start, let's look at that goldenrod ball gall. It contains a white legless grub, a fly larva, which has fed on the inside walls of its snug little plant-stem home all summer and fall, all this time being protected from drying out by wind, drowning by rain, roasting in the hot sun, and being eaten by other animals. This house, the goldenrod ball gall, started to grow as soon as the fly larva hatched from the egg that its mother had put on the young goldenrod, and ate its way into the center of the stem. In the spring, the larva will pupate and emerge as a fly about the size of a housefly, with pretty reddish-brown wings with white markings. Sometimes a gall may have a round hole in it where a hungry woodpecker drilled into the center for a nice juicy tidbit; once in a while it may have a larger hole in it where a squirrel tore a side off.

Sometimes, if you put the goldenrod ball gall in an insect house, other things may emerge, in addition to the fly or instead of the fly. If it is "instead of the fly," your gall has become a "surprise package" like the ones discussed in Chapter XV; if it is "in addition to the fly," you have discovered a gall that has been used by some other creature as a gingerbread home for its young. This is often a tiny beetle.

Neither the mother beetle nor her young can produce chemicals that cause the plant to form a gall. They depend on the gall fly to provide a good house. When the mother beetle finds a goldenrod ball gall, she makes short slits in its outer skin and lays her eggs in them. When the young beetle grubs hatch, they eat their way into the outer layers of the gall. They never get to the center, so they do not disturb the growing fly larva in any way. Many galls are used by creatures other than their makers.

The goldenrod bunch gall was formed when a fly—different from the one that formed the ball gall and from all the other flies we have talked about—laid an egg on the growing tip of the goldenrod and put some chemical there. Because of this chemical, the stem stopped growing. All the leaves that would have been arranged along a tall stalk grew in one little space. In the center of this untidy cluster of leaves, the fly larva lived in a small cell. It grew, pupated, and emerged as an adult before winter set in; then it found a sheltered spot to hibernate, so it would be ready to lay eggs and start goldenrod bunch galls in the next goldenrod growing season.

Although the fly has left the gall, other insects sometimes overwinter between the clustered leaves or in the empty cell. Can you see that you need a different house for each gall in your collection if you are going to learn about gall occupants? Jars will be fine for these houses, but care must be taken to keep them covered with cheesecloth or similar material, since

some of the gall makers and many gall visitors are
tiny.

A chemical that stops or slows down growth is
called a growth inhibitor. Goldenrod bunch gall develops in response to a growth inhibitor. So does the
pine-cone willow gall.

Pine-cone willow galls grow on willow trees. They
look like inch-long gray pine cones. In the spring a
fly—the pine-cone willow gall fly—lays one egg and
a growth inhibitor on a willow bud that is ready to
open and grow into a willow branch. Instead of growing into a ten- or twenty-inch-long twig with leaves
spaced around it, the bud grows less than one inch
long. All the leaves that would have been spaced along
the twig are arranged like overlapping shingles on
this short space. Instead of growing long and narrow
like normal willow leaves, they are short and broad.
At first they are green; in the fall they turn yellow,
then brown, and eventually gray. In the center a
round cell protects the bright-orange fly larva, which
stays in the gall all winter.

Pine-cone willow galls.

Because the growth inhibitor was placed on the
terminal bud, that willow branch will never grow
longer. The gall will remain on the twig for many
years after the fly has left it. You can recognize old
galls by their frayed condition and their faded color.
Even old galls may be good collecting places, however, for many insects hide under the "pine-cone"
scales during the winter; others lay their eggs beneath the scales, where they are protected from enemies.

Many gall makers use the galls only during the
spring and summer months. Some pupate in the galls
in late summer and emerge as adults before the frost;

Mossy rose gall.

Blackberry knot gall.

others leave the galls as larvae and overwinter as pupae in some hiding place nearby.

Mossy rose galls and blackberry knot galls are both occupied by their makers all through the winter months. A mossy rose gall looks like a tangled mass of threads on the branch of a rose bush. If you cut through the mass, you will discover dozens or even hundreds of small hard cells. Each cell contains one small white wasp larva. The blackberry knot gall is a knobby, hard, woody growth on blackberry stems. It, too, contains many cells, each with a white wasp larva.

How can you tell a wasp larva from a fly larva or a caterpillar? A good way is to collect enough galls of the same kind so you can open some, draw the larvae, and take notes about them while you keep others to see what emerges from them. By now you know, however, that there can be some extras— some surprise packages, or unexpected visitors—so you must be careful in drawing conclusions.

Because insects that live in galls are so well protected, many of them differ from their relatives which live in less sheltered places. Gall caterpillars have a head and six legs. These legs are on the thorax. They do not have the extra fleshy prolegs on the abdomen that most other caterpillars have. Wasp and fly larvae in galls do not have any legs, so if you find a white wormlike insect with six short legs in the cell of a gall, you have a caterpillar.

If you have a white legless insect, it could be either a wasp larva or a fly larva. These are hard even for an expert to tell apart unless he has reared them. But if the grub is yellow, red, orange, or salmon-colored, it is a fly larva. All wasp larvae that have been discovered so far are white.

The mossy rose gall and the blackberry knot gall are different from the goldenrod galls and the pine-cone willow gall in two ways. They are made of many cells, each containing one grub. In addition, they are extra growths. You could pull the mossy rose gall off the stalk on which it was growing and have a normal stem left.

Hundreds of kinds of galls grow on oak trees. A few, like goldenrod-stem galls, are swellings in the twigs, but most of them are extra growths. They come in every size and shape. Some are hard, some are soft, some are solid, some are hollow, some are smooth, some are spiny, some are fuzzy, some have one cell, some have many cells, some grow on leaves, some on twigs, some even grow on acorns and oak flowers. Some grow on many kinds of oak trees; some only grow on one kind. Most oak galls are caused by tiny wasps that are smaller than fruit flies, but a few are caused by other gall insects.

Oak galls are rich in tannic acid. Until the twentieth century, some kinds were gathered to produce tannic acid for tanning leather. They also were used in producing high-quality ink. This ink was so good that for many years it was the only kind used by the United States Treasury Department.

At present, galls have no commercial use. They are simply interesting structures. Although they do not help the plant they grow on, most of them do not seem to harm it. The one exception to this is the spruce aphid gall. These galls look like small cones at the ends of the branches. They begin to grow when

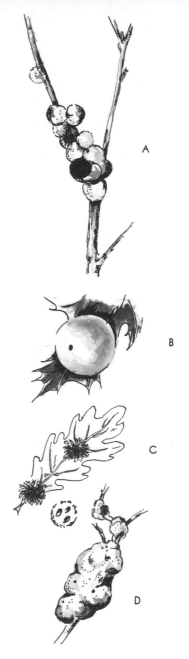

Oak galls: (A) Bullet gall. (B) Oak apple gall. (C) Hedgehog gall. (D) Gouty oak gall.

aphids feed on the developing twig. A little pocket
forms at the base of each new needle. The twig grows
thick instead of long; the needles are short and close
together. Instead of a branch three to ten inches long,
the tree produces a cone about an inch long. In each
little cell a female aphid is feeding. There are no
male spruce-gall aphids. In midsummer the cell
opens, and the aphid flies out. She lays eggs at the
base of next year's leaf buds. The eggs hatch, and
the young aphids all line up at the edge of the bud,
ready to start feeding and making galls the next
spring. Since the gall stops the forward growth of
a branch, and some trees have hundreds and thousands of galls, with each aphid from a gall capable of
laying eggs that start several hundred new galls the
next year, the number grows and grows until the
tree begins to suffer from having all its young leaves
and branches stunted.

In the western United States, the aphid that makes
the spruce gall is called Cooley spruce-gall aphid. It
feeds both on spruce trees and Douglas fir trees. Its
life history is the same as that of the eastern spruce-
gall aphid, except that the females cover the eggs
with a white waxy layer that makes them easy to see.

In winter, you will probably be able to find young
aphids near the ends of spruce or Douglas fir twigs
on any tree that has spruce-gall cones on it. This pest
can be controlled by cutting the fresh galls off the
tree in early summer.

There are many other aphid galls. Most of them
are on leaves. They differ from the galls made by
wasps, flies, and moths in several ways.

They have an opening on one side. Usually there

LENGTH

Spruce aphid gall and black
aphid.

are many aphids in one gall; there are no individual cells for the different aphids. Adult aphids live in the galls. In fact, an aphid gall is often a family home where the mother gives birth to living young, which grow up in the house and in their turn give birth to living young. When things get crowded, some aphids go out the open door and start new colonies. Sometimes they fly to a different kind of plant, and the gall they make looks different from the gall on the first plant. Many aphids lay eggs in the fall. If you find empty aphid galls on fallen leaves, you can frequently find small football-shaped aphid eggs on the twigs of the tree from which they came.

Mites are other creatures that make galls. These little eight-legged relatives of spiders are so tiny that you may need a hand lens or a microscope to see them. Their galls often look like a piece of velvet or felt on a leaf, and for this reason they are called felted galls.

In addition to the leaf galls they form, mites are responsible for some of the witches'-brooms that are found on a variety of trees. All trees produce many buds that can grow into branches for the next year. Some of these buds do not open. If they did, the tree would have too many branches; they are there as spares, ready to take over if something happens. When gall mites start feeding, they stimulate all the branch buds to develop, and the tree produces a big cluster of leafless branches. This growth often looks like the brooms that were made from young tree branches before broomcorn was discovered. Since this was the kind of broom that was used in the days when people believed that witches rode on broomsticks, these growths are called witches'-brooms. Sometimes witches'-brooms are caused by a microscopic plant called a fungus, instead of by mites.

Collecting galls can be an interesting hobby. You may try to find all the kinds of galls in your part of the country that have insects in them during the winter. You may try to discover if these insects made the galls or moved in after something else made them. Or you may try to see how many kinds of galls you can find, even if they are empty. The galls you find in winter are usually well dried and will keep indefinitely if they are carefully mounted.

Some collectors specialize in the galls of one kind of plant. Oak trees have the most kinds of galls; willows the next most; roses and their relatives rank third; and goldenrod fourth. Almost every kind of plant, however, has one or two kinds of galls.

CHAPTER *8*

A Well-Stocked Pantry

You may be surprised to see a honeybee flying on a warm, sunny winter day. There certainly aren't any flowers blooming that it can visit and where it can collect nectar and pollen. What is it doing? Where is it going?

If you follow it, you will find that it returns to a bee colony. The colony may live in a specially made wooden house that a beekeeper has provided, or it may be in a hollow between the walls of an old building, in a space in a stone wall or a hollow tree, or in any natural cavity. Regardless of where the honeybee is living, it is a wild animal whose ancestors were brought to this country from Europe.

Bumblebees, leaf-cutter bees, carpenter bees, and other kinds of wild bees lived in this country before any Europeans arrived here. Indians gathered and used bumblebee honey, but honeybees lived only in Europe, Asia, and Africa.

As long ago as 3000 B.C., the Egyptians discovered that honeybees could be invited to live in specially prepared houses called hives. Some of these early Egyptian beekeepers took their hives up and down

Honeybees in winter.

the Nile River on rafts, so the bees could harvest nectar and pollen as the seasons changed. Later, Assyrians, Hebrews, Greeks, and Romans kept bees, ate honey, used beeswax, wrote stories about bees, passed laws concerning ownership of bees, and sold honey to their neighbors.

In spite of the fact that some of the ancestors of today's honeybees were living in man-made houses and were producing honey and wax that people harvested and used at least five thousand years ago, the bees have not changed their way of life at all. They are still wild animals.

Other animals that mankind has provided with shelter, protection, and food have changed. Some have become entirely dependent on their owners. Some that were fierce have become friendly pets.

But honeybees do not pay any attention to people and people's laws. A successful beekeeper must know the laws of the bees and abide by them. In this respect, the modern beekeeper is no different from the two men painted on the walls of a cave in Valencia, Spain, about 15000 B.C. The men in the cave painting have climbed a rope made of twisted plant fibers and are collecting honeycomb from a bees' nest in a hole in a cliff. Imagine what would happen to them as they hung on to the rope well above the ground if they did not know and understand bees.

The painting tells us something else about these early people. Most of the paintings in these caves are of large animals, like mammoths and buffalo. Some have spears stuck in their sides. We believe the paintings were a part of a ceremony, that they were like prayers designed to help hunters go out and get food for the people. Apparently the Cro-Magnon cave dwellers considered honey important enough or good enough to include a ceremony for its collection in their religious rites.

This is not really surprising, since, for a large part of the history of mankind, honey was the first and often the only source of sweetening in many parts of the world.

Bees not only provide us with honey and wax, but by carrying pollen from flower to flower they are essential to the growing of many fruits and vegetables, like oranges, apples, tomatoes, watermelon, cucumbers, and peaches. They are also essential to seed production for many other vegetables, trees, and flowers. Even though some people today have never

tasted honey, much of their food comes to them
through the work of these small creatures.

Honey is bee food. Some is produced for immediate
use; some is produced for a rainy day or a snowy
day or a period of drought when no flowers bloom.
If bees do not need this extra food, beekeepers can
harvest it for people to use. If there is no extra honey,
the beekeeper does not get a crop, for every colony
must have fifty to sixty pounds of honey to eat during the winter months.

Honeybees are different from all other invertebrates in their reaction to winter. You have already
discovered that most invertebrates become inactive.
Others may move away from the cold and continue
their life activities because they have moved out of
winter conditions. Bees are like human beings. They
change conditions inside their home so that winter
does not really exist there.

The inside temperature of a beehive is around 50
degrees Fahrenheit, even on a day when the temperature outside is 20 degrees below zero. This is just the
temperature of the air in the hive. The temperature
of the bees ranges from about forty-three to forty-six
degrees on the outside of the bee cluster to temperatures in the fifties, sixties, seventies, and even above
ninety degrees in the very center of the cluster.

In the wintertime, bees pile up on top of each
other and on the queen in the middle of the hive. This
pile of bees is called a cluster. It is impossible to determine the exact temperature inside the cluster, for
when the hive is opened so the cluster can be seen,
cold air rushes in and changes the temperature. In
addition, the bees scatter (break the cluster), and
many die from the cold.

What makes the bee cluster warm? The bees give off heat. Some of the heat comes from eating honey, some comes from clustering, some comes from activity. When the hive is cold, the bees move closer together—the cluster contracts. Bees that do not move in, die of cold if their temperature drops below forty-three degrees.

The bees on the inside next to the honeycomb fill their honey sacs with honey. When bees gather nectar in warm weather, it is stored in the honey sac, which is a structure inside the bee's body. When they return to the hive, they pass the nectar to other bees, who carry it in their honey sacs to empty wax cells and deposit it there. But material in the honey sac can also move into the bee's stomach; so in the wintertime the honey sac becomes a food-storage tank for the bee. After she has "tanked up," she moves or is pushed away from the honeycomb by other bees working their way to the center for food and warmth, so there is constant movement within the bee cluster.

When the inside temperature passes ninety degrees, the queen bee lays some eggs. Patches of cells containing eggs, larvae, and pupae are called brood. In the wintertime brood patches are small, but it is important to have some young bees on hand when spring comes to do the special jobs that belong to the young bees in a colony. To raise young bees, the colony must have stored pollen available. Pollen provides the protein necessary for growth and health. If the beehive is in a part of the country that does not have fall goldenrod and asters or other pollen-producing flowers, the beekeeper may help the bees by putting out a mixture of soybean flour and pollen that he buys for the bees. He may also put out a sugar mixture if the bees do not have enough honey stored either because the flowers did not produce enough nectar or because the beekeeper harvested too much honey for himself. If he does this, he must put it out early enough for bees to put it into the combs over their heads in the center of the hive. This is the winter feeding area of bees. If there is no honey there, the bees may starve to death even though there are combs full of honey along the sides. If they move to the sides to feed, the space is not big enough for a cluster one to three inches thick to form, and they freeze to death.

Bees are very clean creatures. They do not soil their nest with their waste products, but hold the fecal material in their bodies until they can go outdoors. The openings of beehives should face south, so that the winter sun warms the hive. When the hive becomes warm, bees hurry out. Sometimes, if the bees have had to wait a month or six weeks for a warm day, the outside of the hive is all splattered with bee droppings. Sometimes the snow all around a hive is splotched with brownish gray. Even though it would be very interesting to see hundreds of bees emerge on a warm day after a long cold period in the middle of winter, it is better to observe from a distance unless you are prepared to send your clothes to a dry cleaner and explain why they smell and look as they do.

Sometimes, if the hive is not properly built, it warms up too fast and the bees fly out into freezing weather. When they hit the cold air, they drop to the ground unable to move. If they are picked up and taken indoors, they will warm up and revive; otherwise they freeze to death on the snow or cold ground.

If you are fortunate enough to be able to visit a hive in winter, you may see frozen bees on the ground around it. These were bees that flew out on a day that was too cold. You will also find some dead bees right around the entrance. These bees died in the hive either from old age or because they failed to move into the center of the cluster and became too cold. Whenever a bee dies in the hive, other bees drag it out.

Once in a while, the winter may be so severe that months go by before the bees can go outside. Then their bodies swell with waste products. Some of the bees become sick. Finally they drop their waste products in the hive, which splatter over the honeycomb and the other bees, and the whole colony gets sick. At a time like this, the droppings in front of the hive are black and yellow instead of a dull brownish gray. Dead bees on the ground have swollen bodies and smell bad instead of being slender and dry.

The beekeeper can tell what is happening inside his hives in winter by checking the area around it. If you know a beekeeper, he will probably be glad to show you his hives and explain what is going on; but you will understand that he cannot show you the inside of the hive until warm weather arrives.

He'll probably be glad to invite you to sit down with a piece of bread spread with honey or some honey cookies while he tells you something about his experiences with bees. As he does, you'll see his eyes sparkle; you'll know from the tone of his voice that he thinks bees are wonderful. Pretty soon you'll begin to understand that bees sting only to protect themselves, just as you would kick and scratch and bite to protect yourself if some giant threatened you.

You begin to realize, too, that the wintertime life of bees is just the beginning of a very complicated and exciting story, a tale so amazing that Maurice Maeterlinck, the Belgian who in 1911 won the Nobel Prize for literature, said in his *Life of the Bee* that bees were exceeded in intelligence only by man.

Since then we have revised our definition of intelligence and we know that many of the things that bees do are instinctive patterns. However, the whole world would be better off if more creatures, including mankind, instinctively maintained a healthy relationship with their environment, carefully avoiding pollution and not only *taking*, as the bee takes nectar and pollen, but *giving*, as the bee gives when it serves as the agent of reproduction for the plants it uses.

CHAPTER 9

Seasonal Travelers

Some invertebrates, like some people and some birds, solve the problems of winter by moving away.

The best known of the travelers to warmer climates are monarch butterflies. Monarchs are handsome brown-and-black butterflies that begin life as caterpillars on milkweed plants. When they first transform to butterflies, they feed on nectar and lead a solitary existence, but as days grow shorter and cooler, they begin to assemble. From Hudson Bay, northern Canada, the Great Lakes, New England—from any place where milkweed grows they drift into groups and head southward. At night they rest on trees. Sometimes there are so many of them that the tree looks as if it were covered with copper-colored leaves.

This flight of the monarch butterflies has been observed year after year. Many people wonder how these fragile butterflies continue on their course undisturbed by bodies of water, by cities, by forests. A few attempts have been made to mark some of the butterflies, as birds are banded, but so far no one has worked out a successful technique. So, although it is known that the monarchs fly to warm places like Florida, and although they can be seen wintering

Migrating monarchs.

there with other vacationers from cold areas, and although they always reappear in northern areas after the milkweed is flourishing, no one knows how they make the trip, the exact route they follow, or whether any of the same butterflies that wintered in warm climates return to spend the summer in cool ones.

So far the evidence seems to indicate that the monarchs come back in relays: that butterflies that started life in Florida or along the Gulf of Mexico fly north to places like Georgia, North Carolina, or Arkansas to lay their eggs; and that the butterflies that finally develop from these eggs fly farther north to lay theirs, until finally some arrive all the way up at Hudson Bay.

We know even less about other butterflies that migrate than we know about the monarchs. Some painted ladies migrate to warmer climates; others hibernate in dead logs, hollow trees, and other sheltered spots. What makes two butterflies of the same kind and from the same region behave differently?

Great flocks of little sulphur butterflies are sometimes seen over the Atlantic Ocean. Some of these flocks fly to Bermuda, but not all the little sulphurs are travelers. Some remain behind, hibernating as pupae or adults ready to emerge in spring and lay eggs on clover and other wild members of the bean family.

Painted lady butterfly.

A fourth butterfly that migrates when cold weather arrives is called the buckeye. Buckeyes are handsome butterflies with brown wings decorated with patches of red. They have a large, red-banded black eyespot in each fore wing and two smaller yellow-banded ones in each hind wing.

Although large flocks are often seen flying south over the sand dunes of the Atlantic Coast in the fall of the year, there are always some stay-at-homes hibernating in sheltered places. It is these that are on hand to lay eggs in the spring in all but the coldest areas. In some parts of northern United States and southern Canada, however, the winter is too cold for this butterfly, and any adults that do not migrate freeze to death. The next spring, some buckeyes that hibernated farther south fly northward to lay their eggs in these areas.

There are many problems in learning about butterfly migration. Anyone who is really going to learn some of the answers will have to solve the problem of marking many thousands of butterflies in a way that will not damage them but will have meaning to the person who captures them. He will have to develop a corps of butterfly watchers.

Can you think of some approaches to this problem? Could any modern inventions be used successfully? Butterflies can fly as fast as twenty-five miles per hour. They weigh a fraction of an ounce. Would this present greater problems than those that people must overcome in studying bird migration?

Most migration away from winter is downward rather than "down south." Invertebrates that cannot stand freezing move below the frost line. Each year earthworms tunnel five, six, even seven feet below the surface and dig out round cells where a half dozen or more worms intertwine like a knotted rope and sleep.

Earthworm.

The grubs of beetles like May beetles, June beetles, and Japanese beetles migrate below the frost line and become inactive.

Japanese beetle grub.

The nymph of cicada, or seventeen-year locust, travels extensively within a hundredth of a mile of the place of its birth. When it first hatches from the egg, which its mother put in the slit of a twig, the nymph drops to the ground, a distance of twenty to fifty feet or more. With its strong front legs, it burrows into the earth and finds a small juicy root, usually of the same tree that served as its cradle. It pierces the root with its sharp beak and begins to suck sap. When the earth starts to freeze, it moves below the frost line. Since it takes this insect seventeen years to mature, it makes the trip seventeen

Cicada nymph.

times. In the southern United States, this insect matures in thirteen years, probably because it does not have to travel as much or as far, and its feeding pattern is not disturbed as long.

The cicada has the longest life of any known insect. Since all the members of one brood emerge from the ground and transform into adults at one time, their arrival is noticed by many people. One seventeen-year period happened to end shortly after the Plymouth Colony was established. The hordes of big insects reminded the Pilgrims of the locust hordes that occur in many places in the world, so they called these insects locusts. Real locusts are grasshoppers, which are quite different from these insects. Cicadas, with their piercing, sucking mouthparts and gradual metamorphosis, are true bugs. Cicada is a better name than locust for them, but by now you realize that with many insects, their common names do not tell who they really are.

The downward migration of invertebrates is seldom observed. You can dig holes in the fall and measure how far earthworms are from the surface for several successive weeks, but when the ground freezes, you will need strong muscles and a pick to complete your study.

If a house foundation or road cut is being dug with earthmover equipment, you may be able to obtain permission to make some observations during periods when the men are not working. In a situation like this you could try to discover answers to questions like:

How far down are most creatures?

Are different kinds of animals on different levels?

What are they doing?

Do they respond if they are disturbed?

Most of the time, however, you will not be able to see below the surface. You will suspect that migration may have taken place because things aren't where they were before. Since you didn't see it happen, you can only make a guess—the kind scientists call a hypothesis because it is based on limited knowledge and observation up to a point.

If someone asks what happened to all the animals that were underground in the summer, you might answer, "I think that they probably have gone to a warmer region." And since many of these animals are wingless and even legless, they certainly would go to the nearest warm area—the one just a few feet below their summer home.

CHAPTER *10*

Around the House

Although most of your winter search for invertebrates will take place out-of-doors, you can almost always find some invertebrates sharing your home with you. Insects and other small animals find attics and cool cellars wonderful refuges from winter's blasts. But ranch houses, apartment houses, stores, restaurants, and other places where humans live, play, and work are all good winter retreats.

In late fall and early winter you may be surprised at the creatures that come to visit you even in a city apartment. A greenish-yellow beetle with twelve black spots may walk up your curtain. It's a squash beetle looking for a spot to hide. Where did it come from? Perhaps it lived in a back yard nearby, or in a rooftop garden, or in a park, or even in a window box, for although squash beetles prefer squash, pumpkins, melons, or cucumbers, they will feed on many other plants.

Black and red plant bugs also sometimes wander into houses. There are many kinds of these bugs. Some are very small; others are almost an inch long. They are true bugs with needlelike mouthparts that

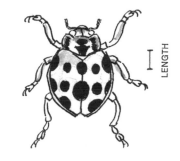

Squash beetle.

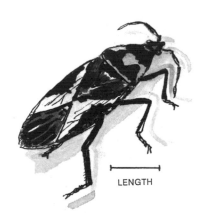

Black-and-red plant bug.

85

LENGTH

Oak lace bug.

pierce the leaf and suck plant juices. Unless they find a potted plant on which to feed and lay eggs, they will quickly die in a warm house.

If oak trees grow near your home, lace bugs may come for a winter visit. If you examine one of these small creatures with a hand lens, you will find that it looks like a grand lady ready to be presented at a medieval court, for its lacy wings look like embroidered full skirts and the lacy projections on the front of the thorax look like a ruff. Actually, lace bugs would be much better off in a medieval castle, where there were plenty of cold, dark corners that fireplace heat couldn't reach. In warm modern houses these little animals sometimes die for lack of food because they stay awake instead of hibernating.

But many houses do have cool spots, like an unheated basement, an outside meter box, an unheated hallway, the space between a window and the storm windows, an attic, an eaves closet. Some adult bugs and beetles as well as a variety of flies can survive in these places.

Almost all the house flies that bother us in the summer and sometimes carry disease are descended from flies that spent the winter in some building. Sometimes a fly wakes up and flies around while a holiday dinner is being prepared. Sometimes one buzzes down the aisle of a store or settles on a table in a restaurant. Unless it hurries back to its cold area, it will not survive until spring. This is fortunate, because every overwintering house fly that survives can lay 400 to 650 eggs in the spring. If all the offspring and descendants of one fly lived and reproduced at this rate, by August one overwintering fly would be the ancestor of billions of flies; by September its descendants would number in the trillions.

Obviously, killing overwintering house flies helps reduce the fly population boom. Eliminating places for the flies to lay their eggs at the end of winter also helps, for as soon as winter is over, the fly is ready to lay her eggs. If there is no suitable place, like uncovered garbage, dog droppings, or other filth around, she will die without reproducing.

In rural regions, where many larger wild animals live, blow flies may also overwinter in and around homes. These large flies with shining blue or green bodies are sometimes called bluebottles and greenbottles. They hold their eggs in their bodies until they hatch into white legless grubs. These grubs are placed on a dead animal. They are part of the cleanup crew of the insect world. They eat only dead flesh.

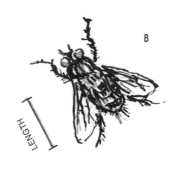

Cluster flies will also be found in areas where there is a park, lawn, field, or forest. Cluster flies are about the same size as house flies, but their wings overlap on their back, so they look narrower. They are called cluster flies because they form piles of a hundred or more in cool nooks and corners. Adult cluster flies lay their eggs in earthworms.

(A) Cluster fly. (B) Blow fly.

Mosquitoes, lacewings, crickets, and ladybird beetles all are happy to find a sheltered spot in your home. A few other insects that normally live outdoors occasionally get into a house and take advantage of the warmth and abundant food. These include carpenter ants and termites. Both of these eat dead wood, but they cannot distinguish between the dead wood of a forest and the dead wood that is used to make houses. They work much faster when they are feeding

LENGTH

House spider.

on the dead wood of houses, for they never have to take time out for winter. Modern heating systems have eliminated winter for these small creatures that live inside houses.

In addition to the strays that move indoors to avoid the cold, you may find some permanent residents. The spider web in the corner not only provides a clue to the whereabouts of a house spider, but indicates that there must be some other creatures around to serve as food. Indeed, you may use his web to obtain information on recent visitors, since the spider does not eat its prey but only sucks its body juices. Is that a dried mosquito or a housefly? What beetle do those wing covers fit? This is the time for a bit of detective work.

A scurrying centipede is another indication that other small animals are available for food. They may be silverfish, sowbugs, roaches, beetles, or insects on house plants. They may be permanent residents or visitors; if they are alive and can't escape by flying, the centipede will welcome them for dinner.

House spiders and house centipedes moved indoors long ago. Though they have many relatives that live outdoors, these creatures are always found in buildings of one kind or another. When a new building goes up, house spiders move in. Often they get there before the owners.

There are other invertebrates that are all-year residents of houses. Some, like clothing moths, bedbugs, silverfish, firebrats, and Pharaoh's ant, have lived in houses so long that they no longer can live outdoors. Others, like carpet beetles and house flies, move in and out of houses in warm weather. Carpet beetles lay their eggs on rugs, woolens, furs, and similar mate-

rials on which their larvae feed, but they go outside
to get their own meals of spirea pollen. House flies,
of course, reverse the pattern and come in to feed on
all the delightful things that can be found in kitchens
and on dining-room tables; and go outside to lay eggs
in filth.

Clothing-moth larva in case.

In the southern United States, roaches live indoors
or out and move back and forth all year, but in the
north, winter kills any roaches that are not indoors,
except for a native wood roach that never has been
associated with men or houses but might be found in
your "wooden dormitory."

Almost any household pests can be reared in insect
cages during the winter. Be sure the lid fits tightly,
for you will not want them to escape. There are two
kinds of clothing moths. The larvae of both are closely
related to bagworms. The caterpillar of one makes
a roof of silk over its head and always feeds under
it. The other makes a case and covers it with bits of
cloth. The life history of either of these or of the carpet beetles could be observed easily. A piece of
woolen cloth about two inches square will provide
for all their needs.

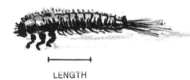

LENGTH

Black-carpet-beetle larva.

Silverfish and firebrats are among the most ancient
of insects. Their young look exactly like miniature
adults when they hatch from the eggs. They do not
have any metamorphosis. Since they are active at
night, they are more difficult to observe; but you can
carry out feeding experiments, and you may be able
to learn something about the size of their families,
how long it takes them to mature, how often they molt.
If you learn enough, you may even write a silverfish or firebrat book, since no one else has.

These creatures will not want a terrarium. They

LENGTH

Silverfish.

Silverfish.

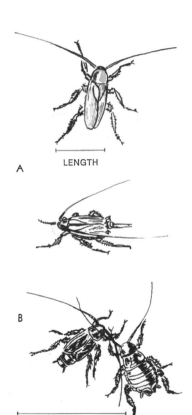

A — LENGTH

B — LENGTH

(A) German cockroach; 1-male, 2-female. (B) Oriental cockroach; 1-male, 2-female.

have been living around people so long that they need their home furnished with people-things—a bit of board, carpet, cloth, or even paper to hide under will keep them happy if you put the container in a spot where the temperature is right. Silverfish like cool, damp places; you'll find them in bathrooms and cellars. Firebrats like hot, dry places; look for them around the furnace pipes.

Although people do not like roaches in their kitchens, they are extremely interesting creatures. They, too, have been around a long, long time—not as long as silverfish and firebrats, but longer than any other winged insects. A roach can be kept in a jar with a screw-on lid. If you take the lid off for a few minutes every day, there will be enough exchange of air. Roaches are active after dark, so you will not have any problem with the roach trying to escape, unless there are baby roaches, which do sometimes wander around in the daytime.

You can make an apparatus for investigating roaches and other insects and small invertebrates. Take two mason jars exactly the same size with two-part lids. Lay aside the flat covers but keep the rims of the lids. With epoxy glue, fasten the top edge of the two rims together. When the glue has hardened, screw the jars into the rims. Now you will have a glass observation house with two identical rooms connected with an open hallway.

Put an insect inside the house. Lay the house on

its side. This is the neutral position. Unless you are experimenting with animals' reaction to up and down, you will always have the apparatus in this position. Does the insect move from one room to the other?

Cover one jar. Does the insect move to the dark end? To the light end? Repeat the experiment many times. Start the insect in the light end sometimes, and in the dark end at others. Does your insect always behave in the same way? Do all insects of this kind behave in this way? Do some move to their favorite end faster than others?

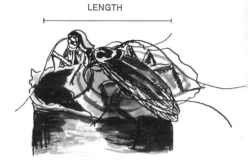

American cockroaches.

Wrap a hot-water bag containing hot water around one room. Wrap an empty hot-water bag around the other. What happens? Why is the empty hot-water bag important?

Think of other experiments you can perform, like up and down, color preference, reaction to cold. Does your animal go directly to food if you place it in the other room, or does it find it by accident?

Does a combination of factors present different reactions? If the animal finds food in the dark, what senses are probably involved?

If each room represents something the animal dislikes, how does it react?

Your experiments will have meaning if you think carefully about the question you are asking and eliminate all other factors. Remember to observe care-

Equipment for experimentation.

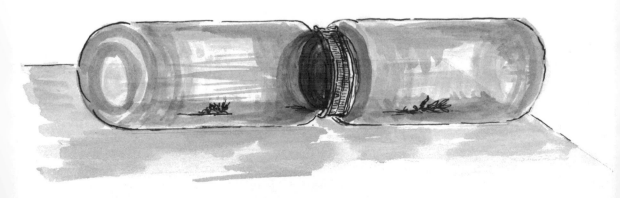

fully. Write down what actually happened, not what you thought happened or should have happened.

If your results differ from someone else's, check to see what was different. Were you working on top of the radiator and he worked on a cool window-sill? Can you find a reason for different results? Repeat your experiments, swapping apparatus and animals.

Results of experiments are never "wrong." The question is "Why did they differ?" Where the conditions different? Did the researchers follow different procedures? Were the research animals different? Examine the equipment. Were the jars exactly the same color? Had they been cleaned with the same substance? Was one of your research animals dopey because of unremoved cleaning chemicals?

As you learn to ask questions and set up conditions so that the animals provide the answers, you are using exactly the same techniques that research scientists all over the world use.

CHAPTER *11*

Business As Usual

You have discovered that the small animals that occupy many niches under, on, and above the earth's surface respond to winter in many different ways. What happens to creatures that live in the water?

The best way to find out is to go searching for them. You'll need warm clothes and rubber boots if you are going into the water. It will be better if the boots are large enough so you can wear two pairs of woolen socks. Several layers are always warmer than one, because air gets trapped between layers and prevents your body heat from escaping.

Rubber gloves that fit over knitted or cotton gloves will protect your hands from the cold water.

If you are exploring a slow, meandering stream, you will probably be able to see the bottom; but if the stream travels fast, with ripples and rapids, you may want to take a rectangular glass baking pan along to use as a water glass. If you push this down on the water surface and look through it, you will be able to see the bottom just as if you were in a glass-bottomed boat.

You will need different equipment to collect animals in the water. A very good device for stream

Collecting screen.

collecting can be made from a piece of wire window screening two or three feet long and two strips of wood each six inches longer than the screen is wide. Fasten the strips of wood along opposite sides of the screen so that one end of the wood extends six inches beyond the top of the screen and the other end is exactly even with the selvage edge that will be the bottom of the collecting screen. The wood can be attached by rolling the side end of the screen around the strips and using tacks or small nails to fasten it. If one or two people take this screen downstream and hold it with the lower edge against the stream bottom while someone upstream stirs up the rocks and pebbles with a rake, an interesting assortment of animals may be captured.

If you are going to examine your catch immediately, you will need a shallow plastic dish or an empty aluminum-foil tray, the kind in which frozen food is packed. Forceps, or tweezers, and a pipette, or medicine dropper, with a wide opening are both useful in lifting the creatures off the screening. In some hardware stores you can find forceps that are twelve inches long or even longer. You can also order these from a biological supply house. Long forceps are useful for picking up small rocks in cold water.

Even without these big forceps you can do a lot of collecting by picking up flat rocks in swiftly flowing water and examining their undersides. Many of the creatures there will be small—so a hand lens is helpful. Small forceps and a pipette will be useful in lifting these tiny creatures from the rock surface. Sometimes a rock may have dozens or even hundreds of one kind of creature. You will only want one or two, but you should make a note of the numbers present. One person can count while another keeps notes. A winter survey of water creatures is always a two-person job.

If you have never looked at the small animals that live in water, you may be amazed by the variety of form, size, and shape.

There may be twenty to thirty one-third- to one-half-inch-long stone cases shaped like small turtle shells on the downstream side of the rock. These cases are firmly fastened to the rock with silk. Inside each of them is a brown pupal case.

In the same area you may find tubes made of sand and pebbles, of leaves, or of plant stems. These tubes will be moving over the rocky bottom or clinging to a stone. If you pick them up, you will find that they are occupied by a slender creature with six short legs near its pointed head. The head can be pulled into the case when the animal is disturbed, just as the bagworm caterpillar retreats into its twig or leaf-covered silken bag.

Are these water bagworms? Not exactly. If you remove a larva from its tube, you will find that it does not have any prolegs, though it does have a pair of strong grasping hooks on the last segment of the abdomen. The hooks are used to hold on to the tube. The segments of the abdomen may be smooth or may have tufts of hairlike structures or of branching, feathery structures. These structures are gills, with which the animal removes oxygen from water.

Since you have found a pupa in one kind of case and a larva of the same insect in another kind, you may suspect that these creatures have complete metamorphosis. This suspicion will be confirmed if you find some cases made of small pebbles and sand—with larger stones fastened to each side to keep them in balance—being pulled over the bottom by larvae; and find others fastened to rocks, with big pebbles covering the front openings, while the insects inside pupate.

When the period of pupation is over—in spring for these insects that pupate in winter, and in summer for the ones that are active larvae during the winter months—the pupa will break out of the stone tube, and swim to the water surface, where its outer brown skin will split down the thorax. A winged insect will emerge. This insect will look much like a small black, gray, brown, or tan moth. Instead of scales, hairs cover the wings, which are folded over the insect's back, so they look like a tent or a gabled roof. The insect's long, slender antennae are held straight out in front of its head. This is a caddisfly.

Because there are so many of these creatures in the water and fish enjoy them so much, some of the artificial flies that fishermen use are shaped like adult caddisflies; others are shaped like caddisfly pupae.

Adult caddisflies can be seen flying around lights

in the summertime. Most caddisflies overwinter as larvae, except for the turtle-shelled caddisworm, which always pupates in winter, and the ballast-carrying caddisworm, which may pupate in either winter or spring.

You may be surprised to find a bright-green animal, which looks much like the caddisworm you pulled out of a case, crawling over a rock or on your wire collecting screen. This is one of the caddisworms that doesn't build a case. In the summertime it spins a net and catches tiny creatures to eat; in the wintertime it crawls over rocks and feeds on small plants.

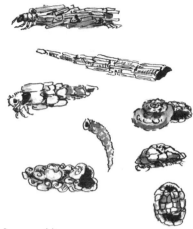

Some caddisworm cases.

Caddisflies have a wonderful variety of habits, colors, and sizes in the larval stage. Some of the smallest of them are called micro-caddisflies. A sandy bottom sometimes has hundreds of extremely small cases that look like spiral snail shells made of fine sand grains. If you are fortunate enough to find one and look at it with a hand lens, you will discover that the little creature in the shell has six legs and a head just like the other caddisflies you have examined. The shell is so much like a snail's shell that it was identified as a tiny snail before hand lenses were available. Other cases are equally beautiful when examined with a hand lens.

Caddisflies are a group of insects that always spend their larval and pupal stages in the water.

The same rock on which caddisflies were pupating or walking on may have had flat gray insects closely pressed to the surface. You might not notice them unless one moves or unless you use your hand lens, because they are so flat they look like small bumps on the rock.

When you look closely, however, you will find you

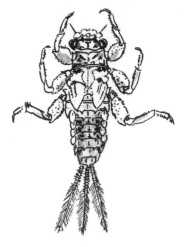

Mayfly nymph.

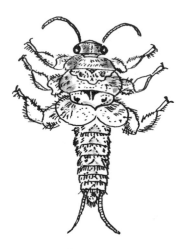

Stonefly nymphs.

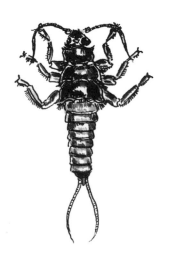

are looking at an insect with a big head, with two shining black eyes, and a pair of antennae. Attached to the thorax are six broad, flat legs, all pointing forward and pressed closely against the rock surface, and a pair of pouches that look like little wings. Perhaps the most interesting structures are the seven pairs of paddle-shaped gills attached to the abdominal segments, and the long, slender projections on the rear of the body. These tails may be smooth or feathery. Usually there will be three tails, but a few kinds will only have two.

These creatures are Mayflies, another group of insects that always begin life in the water. They are said to have incomplete metamorphosis because they do not pupate, even though there is a dramatic change in their appearance between their immature aquatic stage and their adult flying stage.

Immature insects that have wing pads in which wings are developing are called nymphs. Anytime you find an insect with wing pads you can be sure that it is a nymph, and it will not have complete metamorphosis. Mayfly nymphs are even more important than caddisworms as fish food.

Another kind of nymph frequently found on rocks in swift water is called a stonefly nymph. Stonefly nymphs look like flat Mayfly nymphs, but they do not have abdominal gills. Some stoneflies have tufts of white gills at the base of each leg. Others do not have any gills but take oxygen in through their skin. All stoneflies have two tails. These are never fringed or feathery and are shorter and stiffer than Mayfly tails. Stoneflies need a lot of oxygen. They are only found in rapidly flowing clean streams. Different kinds take from one to three years to reach adulthood.

Narrow soft mud tubes may also be found on the rocks. Inside these tubes, red or white segmented larvae of some kinds of the tiny flies called midges are feeding and developing. Like the stoneflies, caddisflies, and Mayflies, adult midges will live on land and in the air when the weather gets warm.

Often rocks in shallow, rapidly flowing water will have flat, round, copper-colored disks attached to them. If you slip one side of a forceps under the thin edge of the disk and gently lift it, you will discover that it is the upper surface of an insect with a head, six legs, and five pairs of shining white gills on the underside. Because of its color and shape, this larva is called a water penny. Water pennies live on microscopic water plants. A water penny is the larval stage of a small beetle.

Not all the animals that live in streams will be found on the underside of rocks. Some Mayflies crawl and run over the bottom. They differ from the kinds on rocks in having rounded bodies and slender legs.

Dragonfly nymphs may be found crawling over the bottom, hiding in mud, or swimming through the water. Some of them are streamlined; others are broad and flat like a dried leaf. All of them take water into pouches in the rear of the body where they have gills for removing oxygen. When they want to swim they eject this water in a thin stream which propels them through the water.

The food-getting habits of the dragonfly nymph

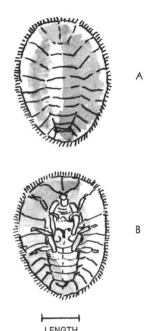

LENGTH

Water penny. (A) Top side. (B) Underside.

Dragonfly nymph with jaw open.

are just as interesting and unique as their travel techniques. The nymph's lower lip is a hinged scoop, which can swing out, open, grasp something, and pull it into the mouth in a flash. It operates like the huge cranes that are used for picking up beams and other materials and swinging them into place in new buildings, except that the whole process is much faster. One moment the dragonfly is standing very still on the stream bottom, with the lower part of its face covered by what looks like a tightly fitted mask. A second later the mask has become a hooked scoop that has snapped forward and grabbed some unwary creature and pulled it back into the dragonfly's mouth. This performance, combined with its spiny body, makes the dragonfly look somewhat like a picture of an imaginary dragon overcoming its prey with a flashing tongue.

Dragonflies always feed on other animals. As nymphs they feed on aquatic animals, including thousands of mosquito larvae in the summer. As adults they catch insects in the air, including many adult mosquitoes. Because they eat so many mosquitoes, they are called mosquito hawks in some parts of the southern United States.

Some kinds of dragonflies take one year to develop from egg to adult; some take two years, and some three. If you find nymphs that are exactly alike except for size, you will have discovered members of one of the kinds of dragonflies that takes more than one year to mature.

Damselflies, the slender relatives of dragonflies, develop from egg to adult in one year or less. Occasionally someone examining a drop of water under a microscope in late winter may find a tiny creature

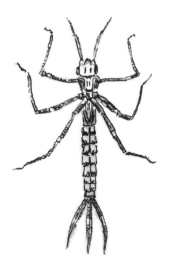

Damselfly nymph.

with six legs on the thorax and three flat, taillike gills which extend from the rear of a slender body swimming with a swaying motion ("like a damsel walking"). The head, with its big bright eyes, short antennae, and that special hinged, grasping, scoop-shovel, face-mask lower lip announces that it is a dragonfly relative. Many kinds of damselflies spend the winter as eggs tucked away underwater in leaves or mud or in plant stems. Other kinds spend the winter as nymphs hiding in mud or rubble and may be caught on your collecting screen if you stir up the stream bottom.

If you want a better look at these insects that live in streams in winter, you may want to take some of them indoors. You will need tin cans or jars to transport them.

Since all stoneflies and dragonflies and some caddisflies are carnivorous, you need to be careful which you put together. In fact, it is safest to put only one specimen in a container. If you don't, you may get home with only one specimen anyway—the biggest, hungriest, quickest hunter—particularly if you do not provide any hiding places by adding some small rocks or leaves.

Furthermore, if you put several specimens in one jar or can, they may suffocate before you reach your destination, for the insects that live in swiftly flowing water need a lot of oxygen, often more than still water contains. In fact, you will notice that your stoneflies are standing still while they pump their bodies up and down so that the water moves over their gills or the thin skin of the thorax, and the water penny floats half dead like a curled leaf.

None of these fast-water creatures will survive in

an aquarium unless you have one equipped with a pump and an aerator. For this reason it is important to return all the specimens you collect to the stream except for one or two you may want to draw, observe for a short time, photograph, or preserve. On the other hand, many of the creatures that live in ponds and lakes can survive in aquariums.

There is a lot more change in ponds and lakes in wintertime than there is in swift streams. The temperature of water in swift streams remains above freezing during the winter. (The exact temperature of the water and the air is something you might want to check for your records.) As the water bounces over rocks and makes fine spray and ripples, a lot of its surface is exposed to air, so it is constantly picking up oxygen. Since cold water can hold more dissolved gases than warm water, the oxygen level is even better for life in winter than it is in the summertime, and many of the animals of the stream go about their business in the same places and the same ways in winter as in summer.

CHAPTER *12*

Ice Fishing

Unlike fast-moving streams, many lakes and ponds freeze in winter. When this happens, the ice makes a tight roof over the plants and animals in their winter home.

Now the only way in which oxygen is added to the water is by green plants, which are producing food by the process of photosynthesis. In this process, plants that contain the green chemical called chlorophyll take carbon dioxide and water and combine them to make sugar. When they do this, oxygen is left over. It escapes from the plant through small holes in its leaves.

In order to make food by photosynthesis, plants need energy. They get this energy from light. In the winter, when the ice keeps some of the light out of the water, plants do not produce food or release oxygen as fast.

As the winter passes, the water holds less and less oxygen because animals and plants use up the supply. Sometimes snow piles up on the ice, and no light gets through. Plants cannot make food. Many of them die. Their decaying bodies use oxygen. Animals are in trouble, too.

Frozen bodies of water are different from flowing streams in another way. Water in the stream is being constantly mixed; usually there is no temperature difference between the top and bottom. But the frozen lake is coldest next to the ice; toward the bottom the water warms up to 4 degrees Centigrade or 39.2 degrees Fahrenheit.

Water is different from all other things in this respect. Everything else is heaviest for a given unit when it becomes a solid. Water contracts and grows heavier as it cools from boiling, 100 degrees Centigrade, down to 4 degrees Centigrade; then it suddenly expands. This characteristic is very important to life. Suppose ice were heavier than water. As the lake became colder and colder and the ice grew up from the bottom, what would happen to the living things in the lake?

The animals in ponds and lakes must make many adjustments to winter. The different species move to one of three places. Some go down into the mud on the bottom and hibernate. Others gather on green plants. Still others are found in the shallow water along the shore. These choices are based on food supply, temperature, and oxygen.

If the lake is frozen hard enough for skating and ice fishing, you might be able to persuade an adult to cut a hole for you so you can go fishing for invertebrate animals. Obviously it would be foolish to do this where the water is deep, since the purpose of your excursion is to catch things.

If you know where plants were growing in the fall and can have a hole cut in that area, you may be able to pull a few plants out with a rake or a long-handled net. If the lake is not frozen, you may be able to do this from a dock or from the shore. Whenever you do water collecting, remember to work with someone and to observe all safety precautions.

The water plants may have some familiar forms like dragonfly and damselfly nymphs clinging to them. They may also have water boatmen and back swimmers.

These two insects are true bugs with sharp, needle-like mouthparts that lie in a groove on the underside of their thorax. They feed on other animals, piercing them and sucking their body juices. They are different from all the water insects we have met so far, for they have no means of taking oxygen from the water. They catch the oxygen as it is released from the green plants. Frequently their bodily activities slow down so their oxygen needs are reduced. Sometimes collectors are unaware of this and handle them with their bare hands. As these bugs warm up, they become active and defend themselves against the giant who has captured them by jabbing his hand with their sharp beak. Although this does not cause serious injury, it does hurt, and many a surprised collector has opened his hand and let his catch escape.

Water boatman.

As the name suggests, the back swimmer swims on its back, using its long broad hind legs for oars. The water boatman also uses its flattened hind legs for oars, but it swims with its back up and its boat-shaped underside down. Young back swimmers and water boatmen look just like adults except that they have wing pads instead of wings. They have gradual metamorphosis.

Adult beetles may also be found on green plants in the water. No adult insect can take oxygen from the water. They either come to the surface to breathe,

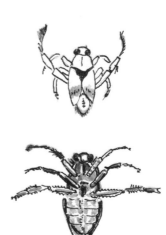

Back swimmers.

Burrowing Mayfly nymph.

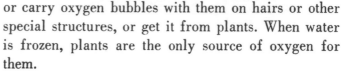

Whirligig beetle.

or carry oxygen bubbles with them on hairs or other special structures, or get it from plants. When water is frozen, plants are the only source of oxygen for them.

The best collecting will be in the shallow water close to shore regardless of whether the lake is frozen or not.

If you pull a net over the bottom near the shore or lift a shovelful of the mud and spread it out, you may find hibernating adult beetles—some of which are ready to waken and take a swim on the water surface on a warm day. Active Mayflies may be found buried in the mud. These are the burrowing Mayflies. They have the same gills and tails as the flattened ones that cling to rocks in streams, and the rounded slender ones that swim through running water; but their bodies are heavy and large. When they are full-grown, some burrowing Mayfly nymphs are an inch and a half or two inches long. If you pick one up and put it on top of some mud, it will demonstrate its burrowing abilities and almost immediately disappear.

Sometimes a crayfish may be found in the mud or buried in a tunnel in the bank. Crayfish live in streams, swamps, rivers, ponds, and lakes. Some dig below the frost line and hibernate for the winter. Others move out to the deep water of lakes and bury themselves in the mud.

If you do find a crayfish near the shore, it may be a berried female. This term is used to describe both lobsters and crayfish that are carrying eggs. When the crayfish is ready to lay eggs, she lies on her back and extrudes a gluelike substance. As this leaves an opening in her body at the place where the abdomen joins the thorax, she cups her taillike abdomen and rolls from side to side until all the swimmerets are covered with glue. Then the eggs leave her body through the same opening. As she rolls from side to side, they are caught by the sticky swimmerets. Soon her underside is covered with a big cluster of blue eggs, which looks very much like a blackberry.

Berried crayfish.

Crayfish are not the only creatures carrying eggs in wintertime. If the bottom of the pond or lake is covered with leaves and vegetable matter, it may be a good place to collect water sowbugs. Water sowbugs look a lot like the sowbugs and pillbugs that live in logs, under leaves, and in other damp places on land. Water sowbugs, land sowbugs, pillbugs, and crayfish are varieties of crustaceans. Male water sowbugs are larger than the females. The females carry their eggs in a pouch on the underside of their thorax. After the eggs hatch, the young stay in the pouch for a while, just as young crayfish hang on to the swimmerets.

Caddisflies with flattened cases made of sand or cases made of plant materials may be found actively hunting for food in the shallow water.

Often mites will be found on the water surface, or running over leaves on the bottom, or holding on to plants. They must go to the surface for air, but they can stay underwater for long periods of time. Although mites are small—the largest ones would be about the size of this "o," and most of them are much smaller—they are easy to see because of their bright

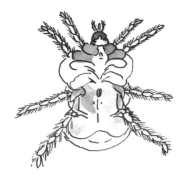

Large red water mite.

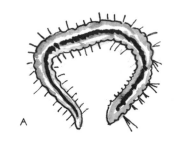

(A) Bristle worm. (B) Planarian.

colors. They are scarlet, deep red, orange, or tan with red dots. Mites are related to spiders, but their bodies have no divisions and are all one instead of being divided into two parts like a spider's. As adults they have eight legs; but when they hatch they have only six. They feed on the body juices of other animals. Often the female lays her eggs on some water insect's back, and the babies hatch out on top of their dinner.

Snails and freshwater clams may be found feeding or hibernating with their shells sealed off or closed.

Segmented worms that look like earthworms and many smaller kinds with long bristles on each segment are commonly found in dead leaves or other plant material near the shore. These animals work summers and winters eating the dead material and cleaning up the edges of lakes and ponds. Like earthworms, they are very useful creatures.

Flatworms are another kind of worm that may be found in streams as well as ponds and lakes. They are called planarians. A planarian has no body segments. It is about a half inch to an inch long when it is full-grown. The best-known ones have two eyespots that make them look cross-eyed and two flaps that look like ears on the sides of the head. These have nothing to do with hearing, however, but are especially sensitive to touch.

Planarians are often overlooked because their gray, brown, or black color, small size, and flat bodies make them blend in with their surroundings. A good way to collect them is to put a small piece of liver on a string and leave it in the water overnight. If there are planarians around, you will have a good supply in the morning.

By this time you must realize that there is a lot of

activity going on in streams, ponds, and lakes all through the winter. If you decide to do some collecting you may discover some creatures that are not included in these pages, for different animals will react differently in different situations and in different weather and climate.

In addition, one chapter cannot cover all the possibilities for aquatic invertebrate activity in winter; and finally, there is still much to be learned. It is just possible that if you keep careful records you may write down discoveries that no one has ever seen or described before.

CHAPTER *13*

Micro-Worlds

Fish eat water insects and other invertebrates; water insects and other water invertebrates eat smaller water insects and other invertebrates; smaller water insects and other invertebrates eat still smaller water insects and other invertebrates. Where does it all end?

There really isn't any end. There are circles and spirals and loops and interwoven relationships. Some of these interrelationships involve plants; some involve the micro-world, which is a part of every body of water.

If you have access to a microscope, you can explore a little of this micro-world very easily. Even without a microscope you can get a glimpse of some parts of it with a hand lens.

A good way to start is to take a gallon jar and fill it with pond or lake water. Add a little of the silty mud and a dead leaf or two from the bottom. Then cut or pull eight to ten dried grass stalks that are hanging over the edge of the water; put them in the gallon jar, too. Take the jar home and put it on a windowsill where it will get light, but not be in bright sunlight, for about two weeks. Scientists would call this a culture—an artificial home for growing microorganisms.

Inspect the jar every day. Does it change color? Can you see things in it? You should examine a drop of water the day you start your culture. You may want to examine a drop every day to see what is happening. If you can see a lot of activity at the end of a week you will certainly want to know what is going on. If nothing has occurred in two weeks, you may have to wait longer or start a culture from another spot. It may be interesting to compare cultures from different places, like a quiet stream, a stream with riffles, a frozen pond, an open lake, or even different spots from the edge of one pond or lake. Put samples of whatever is on the bottom into your jar—sand, rocks, silt. Always add some grass or other plants from the water's edge. Put a label on your jar that records the date you started the culture and the place where you collected the water. Always be careful not to have in the jar any animals you can see without a hand lens.

If you look at a drop of water the day you prepare your culture and then wait two weeks before looking again, and you are fortunate and have a good culture, your reaction may be, "Wow!" Your next reaction will probably be, "Where did they all come from?" Did the dead grass turn into animals? People long ago believed this kind of thing happened. They called it spontaneous generation. Scientists proved that they were wrong, that new animals always come from parent animals.

Two weeks ago, you set a jar of clear water on the windowsill with a bit of mud, a dead leaf, and some dried grass, and now you have a jar crawling, swimming, twisting, pulsing with the wildest assortment of life you have ever laid eyes on. How did it happen?

It is partly a numbers game. If you needed a quarter and someone said, "There is one hidden in this room. If you can find it in three minutes, it's yours," you might still be penniless at the end of three minutes. But if there were a hundred quarters, each hidden at a different spot in the room, you certainly would be able to find one of them in three minutes. Catching a single invisible organism in a gallon jar can be difficult indeed. Catching one if there are hundreds or thousands of them is much easier. Under favorable conditions, some microorganisms do multiply thousands of times in two weeks.

The other factor was seasonal change. You brought the organisms from winter to summer. During the winter some of them were hibernating. Some were lying on the bottom in an inactive state. Some had climbed out on grasses and made cysts around themselves. Some were eggs waiting to hatch. Some were spores waiting to grow into plants.

When their water home became warm, they responded. Plants began to grow. Cysts dissolved, and animals became active. They fed on plants and on each other. They grew. They reproduced. Your jar is teeming with life.

After you pass the "Wow!—Where-did-they-come-from?" stage, you will probably say, "What are they?"

"What are they?" isn't terribly important. You can learn a lot about things without knowing any names for them. You can even communicate with others about them.

You can say, "There's a fantastic creature at three

o'clock. It's white with one red eye and it's dragging two bunches of what looks like blue grapes. Take a look!" Or "You want to see something pretty? Look between six and nine o'clock; there's a row of—of—of something that looks like lilies of the valley on corkscrew stems. Be careful. If you jar the slide, the stems coil up and the fringes of the flowers fold inside themselves."

What do three o'clock and six o'clock and nine o'clock mean? They refer to places on the microscope field. The circle of light you see when you look into a microscope is called the microscope field. If you imagine that the top of the field is twelve o'clock, then six o'clock would be toward you, and the other numbers would be arranged between them like the numerals on a clock.

You can have a lot of fun watching activities, jotting down observations, and making drawings without knowing any names; and it is very good training to learn to describe something so well that someone else knows what you are talking about. But if you do very much studying of this micro-world you may find it convenient to know some names to help in communication or to guide you in doing some book research.

Since relatively few persons ever see the life in a drop of water, most microorganisms do not have common names. Some have never been named at all, and some that do have scientific names have never been studied in detail. However, all of them belong to groups, and deciding which group an organism is in may help you gain more information about it.

All the aquatic organisms that cannot be seen with the naked eye are called plankton. Plankton is from

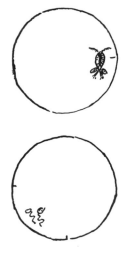

Looking into the microscope.
(Cyclops at 3 o'clock.)

the Greek word meaning "wanderer." It is divided into two groups: zooplankton and phytoplankton. You can probably guess that zoo means animal, and phyto means plant. The phytoplankton of fresh and salt water is tremendously important—not only because some zooplankton, as well as many other animals, from Mayflies to baleen whales, use it for food, but also because it releases a large percentage of the world's oxygen and keeps us and other animals from dying of suffocation.

Your drop of water will probably have some phytoplankton. It may be algae—in the form of long slender strings of boxlike cells with chlorophyll in special structures shaped like twisted ribbons or small ovals or stars, or in the form of little clusters of two or four cells, or sixteen blue-green cells; or it may be beautiful green single cells, called desmids, with a white band across their middle. Some desmids grow large enough to examine with a hand lens.

Almost every culture from a pond has some diatoms, too. These plants live in silica boxes, which they secrete around themselves. Although they contain chlorophyll, they appear yellow or brown because the chlorophyll is covered by a special yellow pigment that they produce. Some diatoms look like boats pointed at both ends. Others are needle-shaped. Some needle-shaped diatoms form stars as they divide. Some are rectangular, some triangular.

Since we are searching for animals, the phytoplankton is umimportant to this story except as a source of food, oxygen, and shelter for the zooplankton.

Some of the green organisms that may appear in your drop of water do require your attention, however. Here is a green fish-shaped cell moving across

Some diatoms as seen under a microscope.

Members of Euglena family.

A

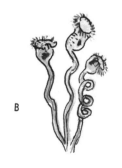

B

(A) Arcella. (B) Vorticella.

the microscope field. It has a whiplike structure at the front end that waves back and forth and seems to pull it along. Behind this is a red dot—like an eye— and an open spot like a mouth. Is it a plant that has special structures for moving and receiving stimuli? Or an animal with chlorophyll?

For a while scientists argued about this. Now they simply say that many members of the Euglena family have characteristics of both plants and animals.

Euglena, and other members of this group that contain chlorophyll, produce food like other green plants when they are in the light; but when they are in darkness they eat like other one-celled animals.

We call one-celled animals protozoa. Some protozoa are shaped much like Euglena but do not have chlorophyll. They cannot produce food. They are unquestionably zooplankton. Often freshwater cultures contain protozoa. The most common kinds in pond cultures usually have many short, hairlike structures on their bodies. These structures are called cilia, and the protozoa that use cilia to move are called ciliates.

Remember the lily-of-the-valley-shaped organism on a coil spring between six and nine o'clock? This was a ciliate with the scientific name Vorticella. A circle of cilia surrounded the top of the animal and swept tiny bits of food into a groove that served as a mouth.

Some ciliates' bodies are entirely covered with cilia. Paramecium, the slipper animal, belongs to this group. Some ciliates even are covered with two sizes of cilia. One size may be used for locomotion, another for food gathering. Some ciliates are so small that you will not be able to see any details even under a microscope. Some are large enough to be visible without any magnification as a dot moving in the water. Many ciliates spend the winter protected by a cyst, either in the water or on dried plants at the water's edge.

When protozoa have plenty of food and favorable conditions, they reproduce by dividing in half. Each half grows into a full-sized animal and repeats the process. Are you beginning to see where the life in your culture came from?

A third kind of protozoa flows along like a drop of gelatin on a warm dish. The well-known Ameba is an example of this. Perhaps you will find an ameba in your pond culture, but you are more likely to find two of its very interesting relatives. One is brown like a miniature doughnut—or a miniature trampoline viewed from above. (Do not confuse gray and black air bubbles with this.) The brown structure is a shell made of chitin, which the ameba-like animal secreted. As you watch, a projection of protoplasm may extend from under the shell and glide forward. This animal is named Arcella.

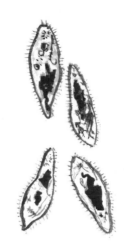

Paramecia.

The other interesting member of this group that is found on pond bottoms is called Difflugia. This tiny animal also makes a shell. It is made of grains of sand glued together with a substance that the animal secretes. When you remember that a Difflugia is invisible without a microscope, think how small the sand grains are. Sometimes a microscope field is full of protozoa grazing on desmid and diatom pastures.

There are many kinds of animals besides protozoa among the zooplankton of fresh water. Almost every successful culture will have several kinds of rotifers, for they live in all kinds of fresh water from the upper to lower surfaces of lakes and ponds, to streams, swamps, and even mud puddles and rain barrels.

(A) Difflugia. (B) Rotifers.

Cyclops.

Rotifers are many-celled animals. The smallest of them are smaller than many protozoa. The largest look like pinheads rolling merrily through the water. Rotifer is from the Latin word meaning "wheel bearer." Every rotifer has two circles of cilia around the head end, which are constantly rotating like spinning wheels.

At the other end is a foot divided into two parts. The cilia carry rotifers through the water. The foot secretes glue and is used to stand on when the rotifer is feeding or resting. Most rotifers have transparent outer coatings through which the grinding movements of the stomach and masses of eggs ready to be laid can be seen. In times of drought and cold, rotifers produce tough shells and lie dormant.

Some of the most exciting plankton animals are the crustaceans, microscopic relatives of crayfish and sowbugs. One of these is Cyclops, a most interesting little pear-shaped animal with a long and a short pair of antennae and a single eye in the middle of its head. Eight legs on the underside are used in swimming. Female Cyclops are almost always carrying two bunches of eggs. The white Cyclops with a red eye and blue eggs is only one of many kinds. Cyclops bodies may be transparent, white, yellow, blue, red, or brown. Large Cyclops can be seen with the naked eye as they move jerkily through the water.

Other crustaceans that are extremely important as a source of food for fish are the water fleas. These range in size from kinds one hundredth of an inch long to some large ones over half an inch long. One kind of water flea is called Daphnia, which can be bought live at pet stores for fish food.

Daphnia, like all of the water fleas, is transparent. You can look right through its shell and see its big eye, two pairs of branching antennae, and ten legs, as well as its digestive tract. Usually you will also see a sack of eggs, for these animals lay eggs every two or three days. In two weeks, one water flea can have thousands of descendants. In the fall, water fleas produce larger eggs with hard shells. These overwinter in the mud.

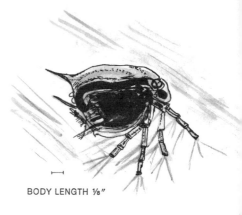

BODY LENGTH ⅛"

Daphnia (water flea).

If you start a culture from a pond with a lot of decaying leaves and silt on the bottom, you may find something that looks like a miniature brown clam in your microscope field. But if you watch, you may see the two shells open and jointed antennae, legs, and tail extend and beat rapidly, carrying the little animal through the water. Since it has jointed legs and antennae, the creature must be an arthropod. If you could look closely enough, you would find it had two pairs of antennae, which makes it a crustacean. This kind of crustacean is called an ostracod. It's an important food for larger animals.

Sometimes the microscope field will be almost filled with a creature with a definite tail, three body parts, and six legs. That combination could only be an insect. You can probably tell what kind of nymph or larva it is, for newly hatched nymphs look much as they will as they grow older, except that they lack wing pads. As they grow and molt, they will quickly outgrow the plankton classification.

Worms, too, or creatures that look like worms, are a part of many cultures. If the animal is perfectly smooth without any appendages or a definite head and is thrashing around in the water, it is a round-

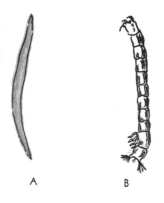

A   B

(A) Nematode worm. (B) Midge larva.

worm or nematode. This is a tremendously large group of animals. They range in size from the three-foot-long Guinea worm of Africa to some of the smallest of all creatures. They are found in every country—in soil, ice, fresh water, salt water, clean water, dirty water. Some grow inside plants. Others are parasites on animals. Many, like the ones on pond bottoms, are useful in converting dead material into reusable forms.

Some people think there are more nematode worms in the world than any other kind of animal, because for every known multicellular animal, there is at least one kind of nematode parasite, and there are also many free-living nematodes, like the ones thrashing their way across the microscope field.

There are several reasons why no one really knows how many kinds of nematodes there are. Both parasites and plankton organisms are hard to study. In addition, all nematodes look alike. They all have the same smooth skin, the same blunt head end, the same pointed tail end. They all have trouble traveling, because all their muscles are in four bands that run from their front end to their hind end. They have no crosswise muscles or circular muscles.

If the culture has other wormlike animals that have segmented bodies, you will need to look closely to decide whether you have segmented worms or newly hatched midge larvae.

Earthworms are one kind of segmented worms. They have no definite head, no legs, no antennae. They do have two pairs of short, stiff bristles on the underside of each body segment, which they use to hold their body in place as they contract and expand their circular and longitudinal muscles to move. There are some aquatic worms that look exactly like small earthworms. They feed on dead plant material and mud, just as the earthworm does in the earth. Other segmented worms in fresh water have longer bristles than earthworms have. Sometimes the bristles are as long as the worm's body is thick. These worms are called bristle worms.

The larvae of midges are not worms at all, even though they often resemble them. They have a definite head. They have one pair of prolegs right behind the head and another pair at the tail end.

When you see a wormlike animal, you will have to determine whether it is an insect, a segmented worm, or a round worm. Young flat worms and hydras may also be found in pond cultures. Since they will soon grow large enough to watch without a microscope, you may want to transfer them to a mini-habitat all their own where you can watch their activities.

Of course, you will have to examine many samples before you find all the plankton organisms described here. Some cultures may have many different kinds of animals; others may have thousands of one kind. Some will have some kinds of animals near the top of the jar and other kinds near the bottom.

As time passes, the culture often changes, as new kinds of animals start reproducing or one kind eats too many of another kind. Sometimes one kind of animal has such a large population explosion that it destroys its food supply and dies out.

There is endless variety and form in the micro-world of fresh water. There are many more kinds of plants and animals there than in the visible water world of crayfish, aquatic insects, and vertebrate animals. There is constant change and drama, and there

is great beauty. There are creatures that could illus-
trate the most spine-tingling horror tale ever written
if they grew to giant size. The whole story of the interrelationships and of the interdependence of living
things can be observed in a one-gallon jar.

CHAPTER *14*

Mini-Habitats

If you are tired of having one eye glued to a microscope you can observe the same processes and some of the same drama by setting up mini-habitats for some of the larger aquatic creatures.

In order to rear aquatic invertebrates successfully you will need to duplicate their natural habitat. This is very difficult for animals that live in streams, but it is easy to make little ponds and lakes. These may be as small as a test tube or a straight-sided water glass. Some of the clear plastic rectangular containers, like vegetable crispers and bread boxes, make excellent larger habitats that are much cheaper than aquariums.

Suppose we start with a test tube. Test tubes have a disadvantage. Air enters water through the water surface. A test tube is like a deep lake. It has a small surface compared to the volume of water. Animals at the bottom will die from lack of oxygen. You can solve that problem by adding a green plant, like Elodea or water milfoil. You might collect these when you set up your mini-habitat, or you might buy them at a pet store or at the goldfish section of a five-and-ten-cent store.

You can complete your test-tube pond by adding a snail. The snail eats plants. It breathes oxygen and expels carbon dioxide. Green plants use carbon dioxide and water in the presence of light to make food. When they do this, they release oxygen. When plants use food, they also use oxygen and release carbon dioxide and water, but healthy plants make much more food than they need. They store it in leaves and stems, flowers, seeds, and fruits. They release surplus oxygen.

If the plant and snail are in balance, they will help each other. As the snail eats the plant leaves, it will release carbon dioxide into the water, which the plant will use to make more food and release more oxygen. But if the plant is too small and the snail is too hungry, the story will end with a dead plant and a dead snail, no oxygen and too much carbon dioxide. If this mini-habitat is properly balanced, you can put a cork in the test tube and both organisms will flourish.

A test-tube aquarium can easily be examined, since the animal that lives in it will always be near to the glass. You can hold the aquarium in one hand and a hand lens or a pencil for drawing in the other. You can watch the snail use its rasping tongue to feed. You can watch the way it uses its muscular foot; the way it lets go; the way it explores its world. You can set up several aquariums with different kinds of snails. Some water snails breathe with gills, some with lungs. Can you tell which is which? Where will each have to go to get oxygen? Some snails lay eggs. Some keep the eggs in their bodies until they hatch, and the snail babies are born alive. If you have both baby snails and an adult, compare their shells. Can you find

Test-tube aquarium with snail on Elodea.

the baby snail shell as part of the adult snail shell?

Hydras may also be raised in a test-tube aquarium. A hydra is a most interesting creature. Almost all its relatives live in the ocean. Some of them are huge jellyfish; others are microscopic animals. All hydras are less than an inch long. They are often described as looking like a bit of string with a frayed end. The frayed end is the tentacles around its mouth.

These tentacles are armed with an interesting variety of structures that harpoon, sting, and grab small creatures for dinner. Then they push the creatures down into the hydra's mouth. Cyclops, water fleas, insect larvae, worms—all are welcome food. Sometimes the hydra catches something too big for its stomach. It pushes it down as far as it will go and lets the rest of it hang out of its mouth until the bottom of its dinner is digested.

Hydras slide on the bottoms of their disks. They also somersault. They reproduce by growing young hydras out of their sides. This is called budding. They also reproduce by growing structures called ovaries, which

Hydra budding.

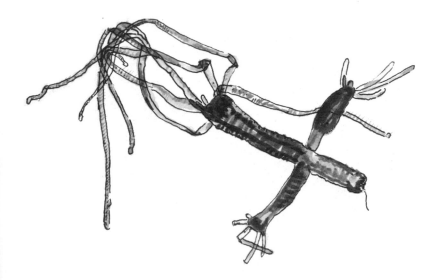

each produce one egg, or structures called testes, which each produce many sperm. Some kinds of hydra grow ovaries and testes both; other kinds grow either ovaries or testes. Either way the sperm swims through the water to unite with an egg in an ovary and start a new hydra.

To keep your hydras healthy you must keep them supplied with fresh pond water. They need food every other day. This can be some of the plankton from your pond culture. Hydras like cool weather. If the water gets too warm, they will die. You may want to keep them in a test tube for a while, then move them to a larger container that will not heat up as fast.

Some other animals that might be grown successfully in mini-habitats are crayfish, planaria, or any of the pond insects, like dragonfly nymphs, damselfly nymphs, Mayfly nymphs, beetles, or caddisfly larvae.

A good mini-habitat can be made in a square battery jar or a rectangular plastic vegetable crisper. Put about an inch of mud on the bottom. Cover it with fine sand. Plant some Elodea, eel grass, or water milfoil at one end, getting the roots down into the mud. Lay a piece of paper over this. Pour clean pond water gently onto the paper. The paper will float on the surface as you pour and keep the force of the water from disturbing the plants and mud.

You could put a snail or two and a dragonfly nymph in an aquarium like this. The snails would live on the plants and would help keep the green algae from growing on the sides. They would be too big for the nymph to eat, even though the nymph would need live food. If you have a good pond culture, this could provide food for the nymph; or you might

ENLARGED FIFTY TIMES

Dragonfly head and mouth.

feed it some terrestrial creature. The dragonfly doesn't care what it eats as long as its food seems alive. You could experiment with a tiny piece of hamburger on a moving thread. But if the dragonfly is willing to eat this way, you must decide if you are willing to go on feeding it this way day after day.

Watching the dragonfly stalk and catch its prey can be an interesting experience. Watching it swim by jet propulsion is also fascinating. To get a better demonstration of its breathing and jet propulsion you can put a nymph in a shallow dish with just enough water to cover its body. Put a drop of food color behind it. Watch the water currents move in and out. What does the nymph do if you gently prod it? What happens to the water?

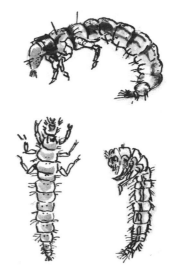

Caddisworms out of their cases.

Mayfly nymphs that come from the mud of the pond need some of this same mud in the aquarium bottom, since they feed on the diatoms that grow there.

Pond caddisflies may be feeding on plants or animals. You can discover what is right for your varieties by observation and experimentation.

It can be very interesting to take a caddisworm out of its case and put it in a shallow pan with case building materials. How does it build a new case? Where does it start? Does it take the material nearest it or does it make a selection? If you have plant material and sand and scraps of paper and plastic, does it select all the same materials? Does it use the same materials that it used in its original case? Do different kinds of caddisworms respond to this situation in the same way?

The same kind of aquarium that makes a mini-habitat for insects can be used for two or three crayfish.

But crayfish need mud to tunnel into, or grottoes of rocks, or of curved pieces of tile, or of broken flower pots to hide under.

Since crayfish are large animals, they often uproot and damage the plants. They can be kept without plants, but their water will have to be changed more frequently.

It is a good idea to lift them out of their aquarium and feed them in another container. They will eat things like insects, earthworms, canned tuna fish, hamburger, dog food. In the wild they eat plants and animals as well as dead things. They should be fed once a week.

If you have a berried crayfish, you can watch the young develop. When do the eggs hatch? How do the young look? What do they do? Do they change slowly or suddenly? Keep a daily record, but avoid touching them. How do they feed? When does all this change?

Can you teach the crayfish to respond to signals? How do crayfish move?

Planarians are other animals that are good for observation and experimentation. They need plenty of oxygen and cool water. During the day they will hide on the underside of rocks. You can turn a rock over and watch the animals move with a combination of muscular action and beating of the cilia that cover their undersides. Like snails, planarians secrete mucus on which to move. They cannot swim through the water. Instead, they climb up the sides of the container. When they are at the top of the water, they can move upside down on the underside of the surface film. When they want to return to the bottom, they slide down a thread of mucus like an inchworm dangling on a cord of silk.

Planarian pinching in.

The mouth of a planarian is in the middle of the undersurface of its body. Just inside the mouth is a strong muscular tube called a pharynx, which the planarian can extend. By pushing the pharynx against its food, the planarian tears it to microscopic bits, which it sucks into its digestive cavity.

Planarians can go for long periods of time without food. They keep getting smaller and smaller, but they remain active.

Well-fed planarians sometimes reproduce by breaking into two. You can tell when this is going to happen because a narrow area will begin to develop behind the pharynx until finally the head end and the tail end are connected only by a thin bridge, which breaks. The head end moves away and grows a new tail. The tail end grows a new head and pharynx. You can experiment with this by cutting specimens in half with a single-edged razor blade or a sharp knife, or you can put them on a piece of wet paper and cut the paper and the planarian both with a pair of sharp scissors. If a planarian is cut in six pieces, it will become six planarians. If you put each piece in a separate container and mark it so you know which was head, next-to-head, and so forth, you can find out if different parts grow with different speeds. Does it matter if the planarian is cut crosswise or lengthwise?

If you want your planarians to grow, you should feed them once or twice a week. You can give them a small piece of meat, or liver, or an earthworm. Planarians will eat snails, so snails and planarians cannot live in the same mini-habitat. After you feed your planarians, you will have to change the water.

It is always better to put pond animals into pond water, but if this is impossible you should draw tap water and let it stand in an open container for three days so that the chlorine and other chemicals will evaporate. It is best to empty your aquarium with a siphon. Remember to put a piece of paper in the aquarium, on which to pour water.

As you get acquainted with the creatures of the world of ponds and streams, you will undoubtedly think of other questions to ask, other experiments to try. You may find yourself going back to peer under the ice, to collect some more evidence about this crowded world where half the residents are going about their business as usual and the other half are hibernating or waiting in eggs and cysts for warm weather.

CHAPTER 15

Surprise Packages

By now you are aware of the great variety of forms and behavior that exists among the small invertebrate animals and especially among insects. Have you noticed how often words like "most," "many," "some," "generally," "often," and "a few"—and how seldom words like "all" or "always"—have been used in this book?

Nonetheless, if you have a chrysalis of a swallowtail butterfly by itself in a covered jar, you will probably be surprised if a handsome, black-winged red wasp about four fifths of an inch long emerges from the chrysalis. Even if you didn't see it emerge, you will know that that is what happened, for the chrysalis will be empty, with a round hole on one side. How did it happen? You were sure it was a butterfly chrysalis.

And you may be surprised, confused, or disappointed if you are waiting for beautiful moths to emerge from Cecropia cocoons and you discover one container has twenty-five or thirty small black wasps with short, sharp ovipositors sticking out of the rear of their bodies, or a yellow-and-black wasp

Empty swallowtail-butterfly chrysalis, after Trogini wasp has emerged.

131

that looks like a yellow jacket until you notice its swollen hind legs, or a half dozen or more flies that could easily be confused with houseflies except for their broad, hairy abdomens.

Even though you may be disappointed not to have a beautiful butterfly or moth, you will have discovered some very interesting creatures.

It has been estimated that over half of the insects of the world are predators or parasites. Predators stalk their prey and eat it—like a lion in a jungle, or a ladybird beetle in an aphid colony, or a dragonfly swooping down over a pond for mosquitoes. Parasites, on the other hand, live in or on another creature, which we call the parasite's host.

Many insect parasites live on other insects. In fact, some are very important in keeping destructive insects in check.

Some insect parasites feed on many different hosts; others feed on only one host. Some insects are parasitized by many different parasites; others may be victims of a few or even of only one kind of parasite. Some parasites are eaten by other parasites.

Long ago, someone wrote a little rhyme that tells the story of parasites:

> Great fleas have little fleas
> Upon their backs to bite 'em,
> And little fleas have lesser fleas,
> And so ad infinitum.

Fleas are one kind of parasite. Scientists call them ectoparasites. *Ecto* comes from a Greek word meaning "outside." Ectoparasites live on the outside of their hosts.

Parasites that live inside their host are called endoparasites. (The Greek word *endon* means "within.") Most of the parasites that you may discover on a winter search party will be endoparasites.

Let's look at that black swallowtail-butterfly chrysalis. How could a wasp possibly have got inside it without leaving any mark?

To find the answer to this question, we have to go back to the summer when the handsome green-and-black-striped caterpillar was feeding on the leaves of carrot, parsley, parsnip, Queen Anne's lace, or some other member of the parsnip family. Suddenly a red wasp with black wings darted down and settled on its back. The caterpillar extended its orange scent horns and thrashed about, but the wasp was not disturbed. She hung on tightly while she pierced the caterpillar's skin with her needlelike ovipositor and deposited one egg in the caterpillar's body. Then she flew away to lay other eggs in other swallowtail caterpillars.

The puncture wound healed quickly, just as your skin does when you get an injection. The caterpillar went on feeding and growing. Inside its body, the egg lay protected.

Eventually, the egg hatched into a legless, eyeless grub. It drank a bit of caterpillar blood, it ate a bit of fat, but it never took a bite out of the caterpillar's muscle or any of its organs. It grew slowly, so slowly that it didn't disturb the caterpillar one bit; and it was just a tiny grub when the caterpillar was ready to pupate. But the minute the caterpillar changed into a chrysalis, the little grub changed its habits. It began to eat as though it had been starving for many weeks. It ate fast. It ate every part of the chrysalis but the tough skin, and as it ate, it grew and molted. Finally it was ready to pupate.

By now you know the rest of the story. It molted
for the last time; it was a pupa inside the empty
swallowtail-chrysalis skin. In the spring, it emerged
to fly away, mate, and start another generation of
Trogini wasps in swallowtail caterpillars. Since the
outside chrysalis skin was not a part of the wasp's
body, it did not crack down the thorax as it would
have done had the butterfly emerged, so the wasp had
to chew a hole through the skin to escape. Round
holes in the sides of pupa cases always tell the story
of a parasite.

The Trogini wasps and little wasps that are found
in the Cecropia cocoons both belong to the family of
ichneumon wasps. There are more than six thousand
different members of this family in the United States.
Thousands of other kinds live in other parts of the
world. All of them parasitize other insects. Many are
very important in controlling serious insect pests.
Some are an inch or two long; others are tiny.

The small wasps from the Cecropia cocoon have no
common name. Entomologists, the people who specialize in studying insects, call them *Agrothereutes ex-
trematis*. Very few other people know they exist. The
female wasp is sensitive to the smell of freshly spun
Cecropia silk. When she smells a Cecropia caterpillar
spinning a cocoon, she flies to the spot in a hurry
and lays about thirty eggs in the caterpillar.

The caterpillar finishes the cocoon and turns into a
pupa. After that the story is like the story of the Trogini wasp in the swallowtail chrysalis—except that
thirty little grubs are feeding in the pupa skin instead
of one larger one.

Another member of the ichneumon family parasitizes any one of the big silkworms. The larva of

this wasp lives in the caterpillar's body without disturbing it until it has spun the cocoon. Then it feeds
so rapidly that the caterpillar never turns into a pupa.
Soon the wasp grub is full-grown. It spins a thick,
dark-brown cocoon inside the caterpillar cocoon.
When you think of the tough, layered cocoons the
silk moths made you can see that this wasp is very
well protected through the winter. In the spring, it
emerges as a handsome black wasp with a narrow
waist and long antennae. It is over an inch long.

Aphid with hole made by
chalcid wasp.

The wasp that looks like a yellow jacket with fat
hind legs belongs to the family of wasps known as
chalcids. Although there are a few large chalcids,
most chalcids are small. Some are so tiny they can
hardly be seen without a microscope. Some of the
small chalcids feed on a single insect egg, or an aphid,
or a scale insect. If you find an aphid skin with a
round hole in the abdomen, or a scale insect with a
round hole in the middle of its waxy scale, you will
be able to say, "A chalcid was here."

Not all the tiny chalcids feed on eggs or small insects. Some feed on large insects. Some of the tiny
chalcids that parasitize large insects have another
surprising characteristic. The female lays one egg in
the host. This egg divides into many eggs in a process
called polyembryony.

In 1922, Dr. Leiby of Cornell University made a
study of the caterpillar that makes the spindle gall
on goldenrod. He found that it was often parasitized
by a chalcid wasp. A moth laid her egg on the goldenrod plant in the fall. Then the chalcid wasp sat on
the moth egg, gently pierced it, and put one tiny wasp
egg in it. While the moth egg developed into a caterpillar, the one chalcid wasp egg broke into over a

Spindle gall with chalcid holes.

hundred eggs. When the gall formed around the caterpillar, over one hundred wasp eggs were ready to hatch in its body. You are not likely to discover this chalcid unless you make a study of goldenrod galls. But if you find a spindle gall with many tiny holes instead of one large one, you can be sure that scores of chalcid wasps came out of there.

You might have collected some chalcid wasp larvae when you went ice fishing, for some kinds of chalcids wrap their wings around their bodies and swim down into the water to lay their eggs in caddisfly larva.

Some parasites have developed special ways of getting around. A small wasp that parasitizes praying-mantis eggs flies around until she finds a female mantis. She settles down on the mantis's back in some protected spot, like the area under a wing, and tears her own wings off. She becomes an ectoparasite, but when the mantis starts forming her frothy egg case, she crawls off her host into the froth. There she deposits her eggs in the mantis eggs; then she hurries back to her host. Of course, when the mantis dies at the onset of winter, she, too, dies; but she has provided food and winter shelter for her young.

The life processes of parasites follow the life history of the host. If the parasite emerged when the host was not available, she would have no place to lay her eggs. If the embryo killed the host before it (the parasite) was ready to transform into an adult, it would be trapped in the host's dead body without any food.

Many sphinx caterpillars are parasitized by small wasps called braconids, which belong to the ichneumon family. If you find a dried caterpillar skin covered with a hundred or more tiny white silken cocoons that look like small grains of rice, you will

Caterpillar of sphinx moth, with cocoons of braconid wasp.

have discovered the pupating stage of an important natural insecticide. Sometimes clusters of these cocoons can be found attached to leaves and stems, for there are many species of braconid wasps that feed on the many species of sphinx caterpillars.

All of them emerge from the caterpillar just before it dies; then they spin their cocoons. When there are a lot of sphinx caterpillars around, then there also are a lot of sphinx-eating braconid wasps. After a while they kill so many caterpillars that there are none around in which to lay their eggs; then the number of braconid wasps drops off. There are hundreds of kinds of sphinx caterpillars. Very few of them are problems. The adult moths add beauty to our world and help pollinate flowers. The larvae do not reach numbers large enough to damage crops. We can thank the tiny braconid wasps for this happy balance.

Wasps are not the only insect parasites. The larvae of many species of flies also are parasites. Some parasitic flies are large, like the ones that emerged from our imaginary Cecropia cocoon, or even as large as a bee. Others are tiny, as small as the chalcids and braconids. In fact, unless you have a microscope, so you can see the four wings and slender abdomen of the wasps, and the two wings with a pair of halteres and the broader abdomen of the fly, you will have a difficult time telling these mini-insects apart.

Some of the eggs found on the bark of trees are eggs of the small-headed fly. The larva of this fly lives on spiders. The adult lays thousands of eggs. If a spider happens to walk by when the little grubs hatch, one hitchhikes a ride and bores into its skin. Now the story is reversed. The fly eats the spider! Another fly lays its eggs in the egg case of the spider.

We've already encountered cluster flies piled in

sheltered corners while they wait for spring to go out
to parasitize earthworms.

Because so much parasite activity is "undercover
work," there is much that we do not know. Most of
the parasites described here are common ones. If you
find other kinds, you might write about them to the
entomology department of your state university.

Sometimes parasites have been brought from other
countries to help combat insect pests. Sometimes this
has worked well, but sometimes it doesn't work at all
because the parasite must be on a schedule of develop-
ment that fits the schedule of its host. Sometimes the
two insects react to our climate differently and cannot get synchronized.

Spraying with DDT and other general killers
makes some kinds of insects increase. The insecticide
does not penetrate leaf galls, or leaf mines, or tree
trunks, but it does kill the wasps that use their ovipositors to penetrate the plants, leaves, and wood with
natural insect controls.

As you get to know parasites, you will begin to
appreciate the complexities and the wonderful interrelationships of the natural world.

You will not be as perplexed as some sixth graders
in a New York City school were when they found about
thirty cocoons under the granite trim on the outside
of their building. On the outside, the cocoons all
looked alike. Some, however, contained the sculptured
pupa cases of moths; in others, the case was broken
and a smooth brown oval puparium of a fly occupied the space; and in still others, the puparium was
broken and several rice-grain-shaped silken cocoons
filled the area.

Could you reconstruct the story from this evidence?

CHAPTER *16*

Creatures of the Snow

After studying insects for a while, you may begin to think that nothing they do can surprise you. But suppose you were walking through the woods or over a vacant lot and you saw a patch of black or green or gray snow ahead of you. You hurry to examine it and find that this "colored snow" is very much alive, jumping and hopping in all directions. Then you examine it with a hand lens and find that you are looking at hundreds of tiny insects. Wouldn't you be a bit surprised?

Or suppose you saw some creatures with long, slender legs, looking much like daddy longlegs, crawl up from a snowdrift, mate, and return to the depths of the snow. Wouldn't you wonder if your eyes had played tricks on you?

If you were studying small animals in a stream and you found some of the stonefly nymphs crawling up on the bank, shedding their skins, and emerging as winged adults, wouldn't you think they had got their calendars confused?

After all, fresh water freezes at 32 degrees Fahrenheit. Water below the ice and in flowing streams is a lot warmer than the air during real wintry

Snow fleas or springtails.

weather. When these animals, whose body temperatures supposedly drops with the temperature of their surroundings, appear on the snow surface in freezing weather, of course you're surprised and will ask questions.

Who are they?

Why do they behave this way?

How do they function in freezing weather?

The answers to many of the questions that these insects raise have not yet been discovered.

We don't know why a small group of stoneflies emerge, mate, and lay eggs in winter, and all the hundreds of other kinds must wait for warm weather; or how tiny snow fleas skip over snow, water, and other icy surfaces in temperatures that make warm-blooded animals seek shelter and human collectors' teeth chatter!

We know they behave the way they do because of a built-in inherited characteristic. We know that the number of insects that can function on the earth's surface in winter is small—less than a millionth of all the existing kinds of insects.

Nonetheless, if you are really interested in meeting these creatures of the snow, you can probably find some of them. The best place to start is along the bank of a swift-flowing stream in January, February, or early March. There you may meet one or more kinds of winter stoneflies. If you can only make one trip, February is the best month, because the early kinds that start emerging in January will still be around, and those that appear in February and March may have started coming out.

The best known of the winter stoneflies has the scientific name of *Capnia pygmea*, which means "smoky

dwarf." This is a good description. *Capnia pygmea*
is a dark-gray insect, less than half an inch long.
When farmers in the eastern United States worked
in their woods during the winter, they often saw
these small creatures climbing over the snow and they
named them the snowflies. In the western United States,
a closely related stonefly (*Capnia vivipara*) is called
the winter stonefly.

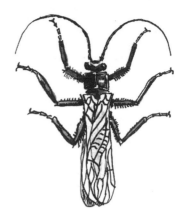

Stonefly.

Stoneflies that emerge in winter reach their full
size as nymphs during the coldest days of the year;
but they pay no attention to the temperature. When
their last nymphal skin is tight, they move toward
the stream bank and climb out on land. They clamber
over the snow, over ice, over fallen logs, over rocks.
Somewhere along the way they stop; their nymphal
skin splits down the back of the thorax and the adult
insect pulls itself free. At first the adult is soft and
light in color; but gradually its wings unfold, its
body hardens and darkens. It walks away from its
molted skin—up, up, up, away from the stream bank,
up rocks, up buildings, up tree trunks. Often it feeds
on green algae much like the green algae it ate in
the water.

Males and females mate. Females return to the water to lay their eggs. Sometimes they fly back; sometimes they crawl back.

The male winter stoneflies of the West never develop
wings. Some of the females have full-length wings;
others have short wings. But even the kinds of stoneflies that have full-sized wings do not fly very well
and often crawl rather than fly.

The larger kinds of stoneflies that emerge in February and early March behave much like their smaller
relatives except that they eat tree buds instead of

algae. One kind in the state of Washington does a lot of damage if it gets into apple orchards.

Stoneflies are among the oldest known insects. Fossil stoneflies have been found in rocks 200 million years old. They are closely related to roaches and grasshoppers. Like their relatives, they have straight fore wings covering their large hind wings, which are pleated like a fan. They have chewing mouthparts, long, slender antennae, and two tails, called cerci, on the abdomen. They have gradual metamorphosis. Usually they eat plant food. The big difference between stoneflies and their relatives is the aquatic stage of the stonefly nymphs.

The other group of insects that frequently functions in winter goes back in the earth's history even farther than roaches and stoneflies. In Scotland, rocks 300 million years old have been found with fossils of the tiny insects that we call springtails or snow fleas. Pieces of amber from Manitoba, Canada, also frequently contain perfectly preserved springtails. Amber is tree sap that hardened millions of years ago and so became preserved. Insects feeding on the sap or walking over it got stuck in the gooey substance and sometimes were trapped; so fossil tree sap often contains fossil insects.

Springtails are the oldest known fossil insects. Modern springtails look just like their ancient ancestors. Entomologists believe that the first insects on earth probably behaved much like springtails do today.

These insects never develop wings. Newly hatched springtails look exactly like their parents except for their smaller size. They have no metamorphosis.

If you are fortunate enough to find springtails jumping on the snow and succeed in catching and examining one, you will discover that it jumps by means of a "tail." This structure consists of two spines folded forward on the underside of the abdomen and held in place by a pair of short projections.

There are many kinds of springtails. Since they are extremely small, they are seldom seen except for the ones that appear on the surface of the snow and are known as snow fleas. Sometimes these occur in large numbers, so that newspaper stories are written about them and people go out to see these strange creatures.

Sometimes they appear in places where maple sap is being harvested, since some kinds still feed on oozing sap, like their Manitoba ancestors did. Other springtails are part of the earth's clean-up squad and feed on dead or decaying matter.

A third group of insects that is commonly seen outdoors in the wintertime are winter gnats. These tiny flies emerge on warm February days and dance in flocks of scores, hundreds, even thousands, with their heads facing into the breeze. Since the larvae of some kinds feed on decaying plant material in woods, it is not unusual to see them on ski slopes, where someone always says, "Look at that big flock of mosquitoes. They surely are rushing the season." But mosquitoes are different from winter gnats. The gnats dance; mosquitoes bite. They are different in structure, too, although both groups of insects belong to the big order of flies.

The winter crane fly belongs to this same order. These insects are rarely seen, even though some of them may be emerging with the winter gnats near crowded ski slopes. The gnats congregate in large numbers and fly out in the sunlight, but the crane flies

BODY LENGTH ⅛"

Winter gnat.

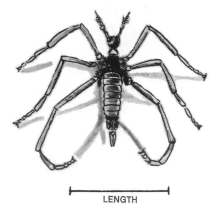

LENGTH

Winter crane fly.

stay near the place where they emerged from the snow.

The crane flies, which complete their life histories in the warm months, look like giant mosquitoes, and they scare people who do not realize that these slender-winged, long-legged flies feed on nectar from flowers and cannot bite.

The winter crane flies have the same long, slender legs as mosquitoes, which break whenever they are picked up. They also have the same V-shaped mark on the thorax, between the place where the wings should be, but they haven't any wings. They do, however, have halteres like their other fly relatives.

No one understands how they can come up through the snow without breaking their fragile legs. They usually appear on sunny mornings. As soon as a pair have mated, they separate and go back under the snow. There the female lays eggs in the dead leaves and other plant material around the trunks of trees.

Because of its schedule, its lack of wings, and its habit of walking over the snow, the winter crane fly might be confused with the "snow-born Boreus," or winter scorpionfly, which emerges from moss, snow, and fallen leaves during the period of November through March. A close look will reveal many differences. All scorpionflies have a long beak, somewhat like an elephant's trunk, with the mouthparts at the end. Males have a pair of claspers on the rear of the body. When they run, they turn their slender abdomen up. This habit gave them the name "scorpionfly," because people thought they looked like small scorpions with wings.

Female winter scorpionflies never develop wings.

The males' wings are imperfectly formed and are not used for flying.

The other name for winter scorpionflies comes from its scientific name *Boreus*, which means "northerner." Snow-born Boreus, the northerner born in the snow, is small, only a quarter of an inch long, counting the male's claspers and the female's long ovipositor, but it can add real excitement to a winter's day, as can any of these hardy exceptions to the rules, which find winter the best time for maturing and for starting new families.

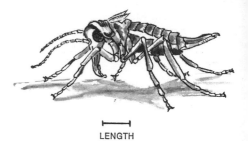

LENGTH

Winter scorpionfly.

CHAPTER *17*

An End and a Beginning

Once you have become acquainted with some of the invertebrate animals in winter, you will find that you reach for a hand lens instead of a can of insecticide when a small insect flies across your room in December—not just because you have discovered that these small animals are extremely interesting, but because you begin to sense that there is a very exciting interrelationship between all living things and that although some things need to be controlled, all contribute to the richness of life on planet Earth.

You look at the insect and think, It looks like a fly. Does it have two wings and halteres? Is it a fruit fly? Or a parasite?

If it has four wings, you wonder, Is it a chalcid wasp with only one vein in each wing? Or is it a winged aphid? Where did it come from? Are there other specimens like it around? Will it live in an insect house? What would I need to feed it?

You'll also see things outdoors that you never saw before. You watch the nuthatch go down the tree trunk inspecting the bark, and you decide to join it with your hand lens and increased awareness—and you discover a variety of eggs and cocoons.

You see a dozen woolly bears walking along a curb on a balmy day in the middle of winter, and you wonder if you are seeing something that doesn't often happen, or if you are seeing things that you never saw before because you have just begun to really look at the world of winter. Whatever the reason, it is very exciting!

Every one of these things could happen, even though they are not included in this book. No book can be large enough to include all the things that we know about invertebrate animals in winter. In addition, there will always be some creatures who behave somewhat differently from other creatures of their kind. And finally, there are many things no one knows about either summer or winter behavior of some of these animals.

So if there are things you think need to be added, why don't you write your own chapters? When spring arrives, you may find that you are hooked by one of the activities you started. Life in a pond becomes even more crowded in warm months. After you have become acquainted with the animals that are active in winter, you may want to return to see what they do in spring and summer. You may enjoy meeting some new creatures that come up from the mud when the water gets warm. You may want to make additions or replacements to your aquariums.

Or maybe you found a moth emerging from a cocoon in your insect house the most exciting thing you ever witnessed; so you decide to start with eggs or baby caterpillars and watch the whole story unfold.

A gall collection started in winter can be greatly expanded in spring, when most galls are forming.

If you visited a beekeeper in winter, you'll certainly want to return when you can see the inside of the hive. Maybe he'll be able to show you bees that are dancing to tell the other bees where food is located. At first you'll have trouble believing any insects could communicate in this way.

Karl von Frisch, the German scientist who discovered this "language" of the bees by performing many experiments with thousands of honeybees marked with colored dots on their thorax, says you *should* doubt it until you have the opportunity to see this very exciting performance for yourself. Even if you cannot visit a hive, you can learn much about honeybees, and other bees as well, by watching them collecting nectar and pollen when flowers start to bloom.

Whether you carry out new winter activities or warm-weather activities that grew out of winter activities, you'll find one discovery leading to another. You'll experience the joy of using all your senses for making discoveries, for witnessing the interrelatedness of life.

What Animal Is This?

Key to Invertebrate Animals

Over the years that scientists have been learning about living things, they have organized their findings and put similar things into the same group. Then they have divided large groups into smaller groups.

Invertebrate animals have been divided into ten main groups called phyla (singular: phylum). Six of these groups are entirely or largely aquatic. Only four of them will be found on dry land.

The four phyla found on land include thousands of different animals. With this many animals living in all kinds of places, you will undoubtedly find some animals that are not mentioned in any chapter in this book. This key will help you identify them.

A key is an organized listing of characteristics that can be used for identification. In a key the information is paired. You have two choices. You decide which choice fits your animal. Sometimes the choice tells you the name; often it tells you to go to another choice.

Key to the Phyla of Dry-Land Invertebrates

1. *a.* Body divided into segments   2
   b. Body not divided into segments   3
2. *a.* Legless, long, narrow animal tapered at
          both ends . . . Annelida (segmented worms)

The most common annelid on land is the earthworm.

b. An animal with a definite head and with appendages like antennae, jointed legs, and wings . . . . Arthropoda

(insects, crustaceans, arachnids, etc.)

3. a. Body with a definite head end with stalked eyes, tentacles, and rasping mouth, often with a spiral shell . . . Mollusca (mollusks)

Most mollusks are found in the water, but some snails and slugs live in damp places on the land.

b. Body a white, smooth tube tapered at both ends; ¼ inch or less in length . . . . . .

. . . . Nematoda (roundworms)

Suppose you find a snail in a log and want to know to which phylum it belongs. You read the key starting with Number 1, which tells you: "If the body is divided into segments, go to Number 2." You look at your specimen. There are no rings or divisions on the outside of its body. You read the B choice: "If the body is not divided into segments, go to Number 3." In Number 3 you again have an A or B choice. You start with A: "Body with a definite head end with stalked eyes, tentacles, and rasping mouth, often with a spiral shell . . . Mollusca." That's right; you have found it. Your snail is a mollusk.

Most of the creatures that you find on land will be arthropods. The next key will help you identify some of them. You will discover that there are more insects than any other group in the key for arthropods. This is not surprising, since there are more named insects than any other group of animals in the world. Because there are so many insects, we talk about them in

A

B

Lepidoptera (Promethea moths): (A) male; (B) female.

smaller groups called orders. Some orders are rare and have just a few kinds of insects. Others are very large.

The largest order is the one to which beetles belong. Its scientific name is Coleoptera. Since scientific names are international terms, Coleoptera means exactly the same thing in Chinese, German, Swahili, English, Spanish, or any other language. There will be many times when this will be all you can say, since there are twenty thousand different kinds of beetles in the United States and Canada alone.

Hymenoptera (ichneumon wasp) drilling a hole.

Coleoptera means "shield wings." *Coleo* means "shield," *ptera* means "wings." Most of the names of insect orders tell about their wings. The names and meanings of common orders are listed below. When you find them in the key, notice how well their scientific name fits them.

Hemiptera (chinch bug).

Name	Meaning of Name	Insects in the Order
Diptera	"two wings"	flies, mosquitoes, crane flies

These insects have only 2 wings and a pair of balancers called halteres.

Lepidoptera	"scale wings"	butterflies and moths

You have to be careful not to rub the scales off butterfly and moth wings.

Hymenoptera	"membrane wings"	wasps, bees, ants, sawflies
Hemiptera	"half wings"	true bugs, like red bugs and chinch bugs

The front half of these insects' fore wings is leathery, the back membranous.

Isoptera (termite); male.

Tricoptera (caddisfly).

Collembola (springtail).

Homoptera   "same wings"   true bugs, like aphids, leaf-hoppers, and cicadas

These insects differ from Hemiptera in having the front wings entirely membranous or leathery—"the same" from end to end.

Neuroptera   "nerve wings"   lacewings, ant lions

These insects have many veins (nerves) in their wings.

Isoptera   "equal wings"   termites

Front wings and hind wings are the same length.

Tricoptera   "hair wings"   caddisflies

Caddisflies look much like moths but they have hairs instead of scales on their wings.

Orthoptera   "straight wings"   crickets, roaches

The front wings are straight.

Plecoptera   "pleated wings"   stoneflies

The hind wings are pleated.

Collembola   "glue ball"   springtails

Since springtails are wingless, a *ptera* name does not fit them. Their name Collembola refers to the fact that springtails have an opening on the underside of the first segment of the abdomen from which two sacs, or glue balls, can be pushed, which serve as suction cups and hold them on slippery surfaces.

In the key that follows, the orders are capitalized.

Key to Arthropods Found in Logs, Piles of Leaves, and Other Sheltered Spots in Winter

1. *a.* Animal with 30 or more legs   2

  b. Animal with less than 30 legs   3

2. *a.* Legs long and slender, one pair to each body segment, usually 30 in number, long antennae and long projections in rear of body . . . . centipede

  b. Two pairs of legs to almost every body segment, totaling more than 100 in number, animal curled in a spiral when hibernating . . . . millipede

3. *a.* Animal with 8 legs or less   6

  b. Animal with more than 8 legs   4

4. *a.* Body long and slender, 6 true legs on thorax and additional short fleshy legs with hooks . . . . larva of Lepidoptera: caterpillar

  b. Body oval, about ½ to ⅔ inch long, 14 legs   5

5. *a.* Animal rolled in tight sphere, antennae and legs folded inside . . . . pillbug

  b. Animal lying flat with antennae and legs pointing backward . . . . sowbug

6. *a.* Animal with 8 legs   7

  b. Animal with less than 8 legs   8

7. *a.* Animal ¼ inch long or less. Body apparently all one part; red, orange, brown or brown with reddish markings . . . . mite

  b. Animal under silk or in silken bag. Body in two parts, abdomen and cephlathorax (fused head and thorax). Legs on cephlathorax . . . . spider

8. *a.* Animal with 6 legs   9

  b. Animal without legs   10

9. *a.* Body in three parts, head, thorax, abdo-

Diptera (blow-fly larva, bluebottle-fly larva).

men. Legs on thorax. An insect   11

b. Body in one part. Animal less than ¼ inch long. Red, orange, brown, or brown with reddish markings . . young mite

Mites start life with only 6 legs; on their last molt they become adult and then have 8 legs.

10. *a.* Red, pink, yellow, orange, or white soft-bodied grub . . . . Diptera: fly larva

b. White soft-bodied grub . . . .
. . . . Hymenoptera: wasp or ant larva

If the animal is white, segmented, and legless, and you really want to know what it is, you may have to rear it to get the answer.

11. *a.* Insects with wings   15

b. Insects without wings   12

12. *a.* Body long and slender without any distinct division between head, thorax, and abdomen; with a pair of short legs on each of the three segments of the thorax   13

b. Head, thorax, and abdomen distinct. Legs long and slender   14

13. *a.* Body flattened; ¼ to ½ inch long. Sides of the seven-segmented abdomen with scalloped appearance. Last segments of abdomen sometimes glow with pale light . . . . Coleoptera: larva of firefly

b. Body hard, shiny, cylindrical; brownish, yellowish, or cream-colored . . . .
. . . . Coleoptera: larva of click beetle

14. *a.* Black, brown, or reddish insects varying in size from 1/16 to ½ inch, with bent

antennae, biting mouthparts. Abdomen narrow where it joins the thorax. Sometimes found in clusters covered with ice crystals . . . . Hymenoptera: ants

b. Pale cream-colored or dirty-white insects varying in size from $\frac{1}{8}$ to $\frac{1}{4}$ inch. Antennae straight. Abdomen and thorax same width at place where they join. Found in clusters covered with ice crystals in galleries in wood. Frequently some of the group will have large heads. Others may have short wings . . . . Isoptera: termites

15. a. Wings covered with colored scales . . . .
. . . . Lepidoptera 16

b. Wings not covered with colored scales   17

16. a. Wings closed, held together above the back. Antennae slender with knob on end . . . . Lepidoptera: butterfly

b. Wings folded over the back so that the fore wings cover the hind wings and the insect looks like a triangular piece of dried leaf or bark. Antennae feathery, spindle-shaped, or threadlike . . . . . .
. . . . Lepidoptera: moth

17. a. Insects with hard, smooth front wings that meet in a straight line down the back and cover the membranous hind wings that are used in flying . . . .
. . . . Coleoptera 18

b. Insects whose front wings do not meet in a straight line down the back   22

18. a. Beetles with short wing covers, the last seven segments of the abdomen un-

Lepidoptera (red admiral butterfly); male.

Lepidoptera (white-marked tussock moth).

Coleoptera (weevil or snout beetle).

Coleoptera (ground beetle).

covered . . . . Coleoptera: rove beetles

b. Beetles with long wing covers covering abdomen 19

19. a. Beetles with a long, narrow beak, somewhat like an elephant's trunk . . . . Coleoptera: weevil or snout beetle

b. Beetles without a beak or snout 20

20. a. Beautiful metallic-green, bronzy, or black beetles, spotted or striped with yellow or white. Head wider than the thorax; long, slender legs, big eyes, eleven jointed antennae . Coleoptera: tiger beetles

b. Beetles with head narrower than the thorax 21

21. a. Black or brightly colored long-legged beetles with threadlike antennae; $\frac{1}{2}$ inch or more in length . . . . Coleoptera: ground beetles
    Ground beetles and tiger beetles both run down their prey. They overwinter as adults, ready to begin feeding on other invertebrates on the first warm day.

b. Many other beetles of different sizes, shapes, colors, and habits, like click beetles, ladybird beetles, fireflies, squash beetles may be found. No key can list all the adult beetles that you may find, even in winter, unless it is a book entirely devoted to Coleoptera.

22. a. Insects with curved, colored, leathery fore wings that end in a membranous tip. When the wings are folded over the back, this tip forms a diamond-shaped pattern. Mouthparts are a

sharp needlelike structure that folds into a groove on the underside of the thorax . . . . Hemiptera: true bugs

b. Insects with fore wings entirely membranous or entirely leathery 23

23. *a.* Insect with membranous or colored wings and chewing mouthparts or mouthparts that can be pulled inside the head . . . 24

b. Insects with wings, either membranous or leathery, held rooflike over the back. Mouthparts a sharp, needlelike structure that folds into a groove on the underside of the thorax . . . . Homoptera: true bugs, like cicadas and leafhoppers

Only insects that belong to the orders Hemiptera and Homoptera are true bugs, although some people incorrectly call all insects bugs, and some insects have common names that include the word "bug." In this book, if there is a choice of names, "bug" is only used for true bugs. For instance, ladybird beetles are sometimes called ladybugs, but since they are really beetles, the first name tells more about them. Both of the common names for the beetles that produce light—fireflies and lightningbugs—are misleading. You will find that different books spell these names as two words, as hyphenated words, or as one word. In this book they are spelled as one word, as are all other words where "bug" or "fly" is a part of the common name of an insect that is not a member of the order Hemiptera,

LENGTH

Homoptera (tree hopper).

Homoptera (cicada).

Animals. Philadelphia: J. B. Lippincott, 1964.

The 47 chapters in the book deal with collecting, observing, and doing experiments with aquatic vertebrates and invertebrates.

Hutchins, Ross, E., *Galls and Gall Insects*. New York: Dodd, Mead, 1969.

If you decide to specialize in galls in summer, this book will give you more information.

———— *The Travels of Monarch X*. Chicago: Rand-McNally, 1966.

The story of the flight of one monarch from Canada to Mexico, with information on a butterfly-tagging project that is looking for participants.

Klotz, Alexander B., *A Fieldguide to the Butterflies of North America, East of the Great Plains*. Boston: Houghton-Mifflin, 1951.

If butterflies are your specialty, you will want this book, not only for identification but for the chapters on such topics as collecting and habitats.

Kohn, Bernice, *Fireflies*. Englewood Cliffs, New Jersey: Prentice-Hall, 1966.

Whether you are a westerner who has never seen a firefly or an easterner who has watched these interesting insects, this book of biology, legends, history, and uses will answer a lot of questions.

Lubell, Winifred and Cecil, *In a Running Brook*. Chicago: Rand-McNally, 1968.

This book tells of the summer activities of the invertebrates that you found in the brook in the winter.

Lutz, Frank, *Field Book of Insects.*, 3rd rev. ed. New York: G. P. Putnam's Sons, 1948.

There are several field guides to insects on the market. Each has a distinct flavor. You will find a great deal of information beyond identification in this book written by a man who found insects fascinating and enjoyed sharing his knowledge.

——— *A Lot of Insects*. New York: G. P. Putnam's Sons, 1941.

This is the story about some of the most exciting of the 1,402 different insects that Dr. Lutz collected in his backyard less than an hour from Times Square.

McClung, Robert M., *Caterpillars and How They Live*. New York: William Morrow, 1965.

The author started raising caterpillars as a boy. Today his young son is enjoying the same experiences. This book on caterpillars reflects firsthand experience, as do the author's life history books like *Sphinx* and *Ladybug*, which are written for younger readers.

——— *Aquatic Insects and How They Live*. New York: William Morrow, 1970.

This book, based on firsthand experience, has many helpful illustrations drawn by the author, as well as suggestions for summer activities.

Swain, Ralph B., *The Insect Guide*. New York: Doubleday, 1948.

This is another book that is useful for identification of insects. The illustrations by Suzan N. Swain dramatize the beauty of many insects.

Teale, Edwin Way, *Junior Book of Insects*, rev. ed. New York: E. P. Dutton, 1953.

This is a book of activities with information

on things to do and ways to do them.

Zim, Herbert S., and Clarence A. Cottam, *Insects.*
New York: Golden Press, 1962.

This is a good beginner's insect guide. It will
help you appreciate the great variety represented
by these small animals. The range maps tell
whether you can reasonably expect to meet a
certain insect in your area. Of course, if you
read *Lot of Insects,* you'll know that some insects
sometimes get very far from home.

If you visit a library or a bookstore, you will
find many other interesting books about invertebrates.

Index

Figures followed by asterisks refer to illustrations

Acrea moths, 17, 20*, 55–56
Amebas, 117*
Angle-wing butterflies, 37
Annelida, 151
Ant lions, 154
Ants, 32–33*, 157
    carpenter, 33, 87
    Pharaoh's, 88
Aphid lions, 23
Aphids, 23, 33, 68*–69, 135*, 154
Aquarium, 101–102, 123–124*, 126, 127, 148
Arachnids, 152
Arcella, 116*, 117
Arthropoda, 22, 152

Back swimmers, 105*
Bagworms, 43*–44, 49, 89
Bedbugs, 88
Bees, 153, 160
    bumblebee, 34*
    carpenter, 71
    honey-, 71–78, 72*
    leaf-cutter, 71
Beetles, 34–35, 82, 88, 153, 159
    carpet, 88–89*
    click, 35*–36, 57*, 156
    firefly, 36*, 156
    ground, 158*

Japanese, 57*, 82*
June, 82
ladybird, 23, 33*
May, 82
rove, 36*, 158
snout, 158*
squash, 85
tiger, 36*, 158
water, 105–106*, 126
water penny, 99*
weevil, 158*
whirligig beetle, 106*
Birds, 15–16, 42, 48, 49, 50, 51, 56, 63, 147
Black and red plant bugs, 85*
Black swallowtail butterflies, 131*, 133
Blackberry-knot galls, 66*–67
Blow flies, 23, 87*, 156*
Bluebottle flies, 23, 87*, 156*
Braconid wasps, 136–137
Bristle worms, 108*, 121
Buckeye butterflies, 81
Bugs, 85, 153, 159
    back swimmer, 105*
    bedbugs, 88
    black and red plant, 85
    chinch, 153*

lace, 86*
stink, 21
water boatman, 105*
Bumblebees, 34*
Butterflies, 36–37, 58, 79–82, 157
   angle-wing, 37
   black swallowtail, 133
   buckeye, 81
   chrysalis types, 58*, 131*
   common sulphur, 58*
   little sulphur, 81
   monarch, 79–81, 80*
   mourning cloak, 37*
   painted lady, 37, 81*
   pearl-crescent, 58*
   red admiral, 37, 157*

Caddisflies, 95–97*, 99, 107, 126, 127, 134*, 154*
Caddisworms, 97*
Cages, 26–27*, 28*, 64–65, 89–90, 112
Capnia pygmea, 140–141
Capnia vivipara, 141
Carpenter ants, 33*, 87
Carpenter bees, 71
Carpet beetles, 88–89*
Caterpillars, 18, 28–29
   black swallowtail, 133
   gall, 66
   prolegs of, 29*
   sphinx, 57*, 136*–137
   tent, 42
   woolly bear, 18*, 25, 148
Cecropia moths, 53–54, 134
Centipedes, 19*, 26, 88, 155
Cerci, 142
Chalcid wasps, 135–136, 147

Chinch bugs, 153*
Chrysalis, 58*, 131*
Cicadas, 82–83*, 154, 159*
Cilia, 116, 118, 128
Click beetles, 35*–36, 57*, 156
Clothing for collectors, 14, 93–94
Clothing moths, 88, 89*
Cluster flies, 23, 87*, 137–138
Cockroaches. *See* Roaches.
Cocoons, 21, 51–56, 136
   Acrea, 17, 20*, 55–56
   Cecropia, 53*–54, 134
   Cynthia, 53, 58
   leaf miner, 56
   Luna, 55*
   Polyphemus, 55*
   Promethea, 51*–52
Coleoptera, 153, 156, 157, 158
Collecting galls, 70
Collecting screen, 93–94*
Collembola, 154
Crane flies, 143–144*, 153, 160*
Crayfish, 106–107*, 126, 127
Crickets, 21, 29–30, 87–154
   field, 29
   house, 18–19, 21*
   as winter pets, 29–30
Crustaceans, 38, 107, 118–119, 152
Cultures, 111–112, 119
Cyclops, 114*, 118
Cynthia moths, 53, 58
Cysts, 117, 130

Damselflies, 100*–101, 126
Daphnia, 119*–120
Dead wood, 31–39
Diatoms, 115*, 127
Difflugia, 117*
Diptera, 153, 156, 160
Dragonflies, 48, 99*–100,
    126*–127

Earthworms, 82*, 84, 87,
    108, 120–121, 128, 129,
    152
Ectoparasites, 132
Eggs, 40–49
    aphid, 69
    bagworm, 43*–44
    crayfish, 106–107*
    Cyclops, 118*
    Daphnia, 119*
    dragonfly, 48
    honeybee, 75
    katydid, 48*
    praying mantis, 46*
    of scale insects, 44*–46
    snail, 124
    spider, 17, 19*–20, 25,
        47*
    tent caterpillar, 42*
    walking stick, 47–48
    water sowbug, 107
Endoparasites, 132–133
Entomologists, 134, 142
Environment, 23, 78. *See
    also* Interrelationships.
Equipment,
    for experiments, 90–91*
    for land collecting, 13,
        14*, 15*
    for water collecting, 93–

94*–95. *See also* Cages
    and Aquariums.
Euglena, 116*
Exoskeleton, 22
Experiments, 29, 89, 90–
    91*–92, 127
Eyed-click-beetle, 35*–36

Firebrats, 88, 89, 90
Fireflies, 36*, 156, 159
Flatworms. *See* Planarians.
Fleas, 132
Flies, 153, 156
    blow, 23, 87*, 156*
    bluebottle, 23, 87*, 156*
    cluster, 23, 87*, 137–138
    crane, 153, 160*
    fruit, 147
    gall, 60*, 63, 64, 65
    greenbottle, 87
    house, 23, 86–87
    midges, 99, 120*
    parasitic, 132, 137–138
    small-headed, 137
    winter crane, 143–144*
Fossil insects, 142
Freshwater clams, 108

Galls, 60–70, 148
    blackberry knot, 66*
    collections, 70
    goldenrod ball, 60*, 63
    goldenrod bunch, 61*
    goldenrod spindle, 60*,
        135*–136
    goldenrod tapered-stem, 61
    mossy rose, 66*
    oak, 67*
    pine-cone willow, 65*

spruce aphid, 67–68*
witches' brooms, 59*, 69–70
Gills, 96, 38, 124
Goldenrod galls, 70
    ball, 60*, 63
    bunch, 61*, 64
    parasitized by chalcids, 135*–136
    spindle, 60*
    tapered-stem, 61
Gnats, 143*, 160
Grasshoppers, 21, 142
Greenbottle flies, 87

Halteres, 153
Hexapoda, 22
Hemiptera, 153*
Hibernation, 38–39
Homoptera, 154, 159*
Honey, 74
Honeybees, 71–78, 72*
    in ancient Egypt, 71
    brood, 75
    cave paintings of, 73
    dancing of, 149
    droppings of, 76–77
    and how they relate to the environment, 78
    "language" of, 149
    sanitation of, 76
    sickness of, 77
Hornets, 34*
House centipedes, 19*, 88
House crickets, 18–19, 21*, 29
House flies, 23, 86–89
House spiders, 88
Housing. *See* Aquarium and Cages.

Hydras, 121, 125*–126
Hymenoptera, 153, 156, 157, 160
Hypothesis, 84

Ichneumon wasps, 134–135, 153*
Insecticides, 54–55, 138, 147
Insects, 22, 152
Interrelationships, 23, 31–32, 73–74, 75, 78, 111, 122, 124, 137, 138, 147, 149
Invertebrate animals, 22
Isoptera, 154, 157

Katydids, 21, 160*

Lace bug, 86*
Lacewings, 22*, 23, 25, 87, 154, 160
Ladybird beetles, 23, 87, 159
    black, 33*
    red, 33*
    in Rocky Mountains, 34
Ladybugs, 159
Larva, 21, 156
Leaf-cutter bee, 71
Leaf miners, 56
Leafhoppers, 21, 154
Lepidoptera, 153, 157
Lightning bugs, 159

Mayflies, 97–98*, 99, 106*, 126, 127
Metamorphosis, 20–21, 57–58, 61–62, 96, 142
Mice, 54
Micro-caddisflies, 97
Microorganisms, 111–122
Microscope field, 114*

Midges, 99, 120*
Migration, 79–84
    beetle, 82
    buckeye butterfly, 81
    cicada, 82–83
    earthworm, 82, 84
    little sulphur butterfly, 81
    monarch butterfly, 79–
        80*–81
    painted lady, 81*
Millipedes, 38*, 155
Mites, 69, 107–108*, 155,
    156
Mollusca, 152
Molting, 21
Monarch butterflies, 79–80*–
    81
Mosquitoes, 18*, 87, 153,
    160
Mossy rose galls, 66*, 67
Moths, 157
    Acrea, 55–56
    Cecropia, 53–55
    Cynthia, 53–55
    goldenrod gall, 60–61
    Luna, 53, 55
    Polyphemus, 53, 55
    Promethea, 51–53, 54, 55,
        58, 152*
    sphinx, 57*, 136*–137
    white-marked tussock,
        157*
Mourning cloak butterfly,
    37*
Mucus, 38, 128

Nematodes, 120*, 152
Neuroptera, 154, 160
Nymphs, 21, 98

Oak galls, 67*, 70
Orthoptera, 154, 160
Ostracods, 119
Oxygen, 98, 101, 102, 103,
    104, 105–106, 115, 123,
    124

Painted lady butterflies, 37,
    81*
Paramecium, 117*
Parasites, 132–138
Parasitic flies, 132, 137–138
Parasitic wasps, 54, 131–136
Pharaoh's ants, 88
Photosynthesis, 103, 124
Phylum, 151
Phytoplankton, 114–115
Pillbugs, 38*, 155
Pine-cone willow gall, 65*
Planarians, 108*–109, 121,
    128–129
Plankton, 114–115, 126
Plecoptera, 154, 160
Polistes wasps, 34
Pollen, 73, 75
Polyembryony, 135
Polyphemus moths, 55
Population explosion, 87,
    121
Praying mantises, 46*–47,
    48
Predators, 132
Prolegs, 29*
Promethea moths, 51–55, 58,
    152*
Protozoa, 116–117
Pupae, 20, 56–57*–58
    butterfly, 58*
    click-beetle, 57*
    gall insects, 61

Japanese-beetle, 57*
June-beetle, 57*
Luna, 55*
Promethea, 52
sphinx, 57*

Rearing animals, 25–30, 27*, 28*, 64, 66, 89, 101–102, 123–124*, 126, 127
Record keeping, 24, 28, 29, 39, 66, 89, 91–92, 95, 109, 114, 128
Red admiral butterfly, 37, 157*
Research, 92. *See also* Experiments.
Roaches, 21, 88, 89, 90, 91*, 142, 154, 160
Rotifers, 117*–118
Roundworms. *See* Nematodes.
Rove beetles, 36*, 158

Scale insects, 44–46
    eaten by ladybird beetles, 33
    oyster-shell scales, 44*–45
    parasitized by chalcids, 135
    pine-needle scales, 45*–46
Segmented bodies, 22, 151
Seventeen-year locust, 82
Silk,
    American silkworms, 53
    bagworm, 43
    caddisflies, 95–96
    Cecropia, 134
    Cynthia, 53
    Luna, 55

Polyphemus, 55
Promethea, 51
spider, 19*, 47*
Silverfish, 88, 89, 90*
Slugs, 37–38, 152
Small-headed fly, 137
Snails, 38, 108, 124*, 126, 129, 152
Snout beetles, 158
Snow-born Boreus, 144–145*
Snow fleas, 140*, 142–143, 154*
Sowbugs, 38*, 88, 155
Sphinx moths, 57*, 136*–137
Spiders, 155
    egg cases of, 17, 19*–20, 25, 47*
    garden, 47
    hibernating, 33
    house, 88*
    young, 48
Spittle bugs, 21
Springtails, 140*, 142–143, 154*
Squash beetle, 85*
Squirrels, 16, 54, 63
Stink bugs, 21
Stoneflies, 98*, 99, 101, 140–141*–142, 154, 160*
Sulphur butterflies, 58, 81
Swallowtail butterflies, 133

Temperature in a beehive, 74–75
Tent caterpillars, 42*, 49
Termites, 31*–32, 87–88, 154*, 157
Tiger beetles, 36*

Tree hoppers, 159*
Tricoptera, 154
Trogini wasps, 131*, 133–134
Tussock moths, 157*

Vorticella, 116*

Wasps, 153, 160
    braconid, 136–137
    chalcid, 135–136
    gall, 66, 67
    ichneumon, 134–135
    mud-dauber, 23
    parasitic, 54, 131, 131–136
    Polistes, 34
    Trogini, 131*, 133–134
Water beetles, 105–106*, 126
Water boatmen, 105*
Water fleas, 118–119
Water pennies, 99*, 101
Water sowbugs, 107

Water temperatures, 104, 139–140
Weevils, 158*, 159
Whirligig beetles, 106*
Willow galls, 65*, 70
Witches' brooms, 59*, 69–70
Winter crane flies, 143–144*
Winter gnat, 143*
Winter scorpion flies, 144–145*
Winter stonefly, 141
Woolly bear caterpillars, 18*, 25, 148
Worms, 119–121
    Bristle worms, 108*, 121
    Earthworms, 82*, 84, 87, 108, 120–121, 128, 129, 152
    Nematodes (roundworms), 120*, 152
    Planarians (flatworms), 108*–109, 121, 128–129

Zooplankton, 114–122